Programs for Asian Global Legal Professions Series II

Challenges for Studying Law Abroad in the Asian Region

Edited by
KEIGLAD

The publication was produced by KEIGLAD
KEIGLAD - Keio Institute for Global Law and Development
Keio University, 2-15-45 Mita, Minato-ku, Tokyo 108-8345 Japan
http://keiglad.keio.ac.jp/en/

Copyright © 2018 KEIGLAD

All rights reserved. No part of this book may be reproduced in any form or
by any electronic or mechanical means, including information storage and
retrieval systems, without the prior written permission of KEIGLAD,
excepting brief quotes used in reviews.

Distributed by KEIO UNIVERSITY PRESS INC.
2-19-30 Mita, Minato-ku, Tokyo 108-8346 Japan
http://www.keio-up.co.jp/kup/eng/

ISBN 978-4-7664-2504-8
Printed in Japan

PREFACE

In 2004, a new law school system was established to train legal professionals in Japan. Over the past thirteen years, Keio University Law School has been striving to develop the wide-range of human resources required in the legalized society of the 21st century.

In this century, Asian and Pacific countries are in the process of forming a large economic bloc, and, because of this, various disputes are arising from the global interaction between people and companies. To address some of these tensions, the best way to proceed is to establish a new legal community for legal education and the training of legal professionals, and to discuss the development of global law within that community.

However, most international education in Japan has depended on outbound programs, such as exchange programs in American law schools. For this reason, Keio University Law School has launched a new LL.M. course in Global Legal Practice, in addition to its J.D. program for prospective Japanese legal professionals. The new LL.M. program permits students to obtain a Master of Laws degree in one year, taking instruction in English. It is the first program of its kind at a Japanese law school.

At the same time, in collaboration with six law schools from East Asian countries, we have moved towards establishing a new global legal community and have started joint legal education program called the Program for Asian Global Legal Professions (PAGLEP). PAGLEP aims to foster global legal professionals who take strong leadership roles in finding solutions to legal issues occurring in globalizing societies. This program is unique in that the seven law schools share the issues confronting each partner school as a result of their historical, geographical, and cultural backgrounds.

It is our great pleasure to celebrate the publication of our second successful meeting in September 2017 on comparative legal education, titled "Challenges for Studying Law Abroad," where we discussed various obstacles to students studying law in foreign countries and identified several measures to overcome those obstacles, sharing good practices and experiences in partner law schools.

Finally, I would like to end this preface by saying that it is our hope the success of this collaboration will mark the beginning of the formation of a new Asian legal community.

Naoya Katayama

Former Dean, Keio University Law School

6 January 2018

PREFACE

Mutual cooperation between Mekong region countries and Japan is expanding and deepening, both in economic cooperation and human resource development. Furthermore, deepening mutual cooperation in legal education will promote establishment of joint programs in various fields of law.

At the same time, however, we are still challenged by the majority's inability to access sufficient legal services due to the legal field's lack of human resources. The dearth of qualified legal professionals reduces people's opportunity to access justice systems because these professionals are essential actors in promotion of access to justice. Without sufficient access to justice, people are unable to exercise their rights, challenge unjustified situations, and claim the State's accountability. Sometimes a nation loses investment opportunities because investors recognize insufficient legal services as a crucial risk, weakening not only the economic, but also the social power of the nation and creating further economic inequality between countries.

Then how can access to justice be improved? I believe that the promotion of legal education is one promising answer, and it will be further improved by strengthening the international exchange of students and teachers.

This book introduces various international exchange programs in legal education of representative universities in Mekong region countries and Japan, identifies obstacles that exist in our current programs, and explores viable measures to overcome those problems. Indeed, this is our challenge in improving access to justice through facilitating to study law abroad in the Asian region. As an outcome from the Programs for Asian Global Legal Professions (PAGLEP), it will be shared on a global scale and exemplify human resource development in legal education.

Isao Kitai

Dean, Keio University Law School

19 January 2018

CONTENTS

PREFACE

Naoya Katayama   i

Isao Kitai   iii

INTRODUCTION

WHY IS IT WORTH CHALLENGING FOR STUDYING LAW ABROAD IN THE ASIAN REGION?

Hiroshi Matsuo   1

1. Advantages of Studying Law Abroad in the Asian Region
2. Challenges for Studying Law Abroad in Asian Universities
3. Obstacles to Studying Law Abroad in the Asian Region
4. Possible Measures to Eliminate Obstacles
5. Constructing a Common Market among Law Schools toward the Globalization of Legal Education

COUNTRY REPORTS

Chapter 1:   THE IMPLEMENTATION OF STUDENT EXCHANGE PROGRAMS:
Some Issues from the Hanoi Law University Perspective

Nguyen Van Quang   25

1. The Context: Internationalisation and International Collaboration at Hanoi Law University
2. Student Exchange Programs at Hanoi Law University: the Fact
3. How to Promote Student Exchange Programs at Hanoi Law University in the Context of ASEAN Integration: Some Suggestions
4. Conclusion

Chapter 2:   EXCHANGE PROGRAMS AS METHOD
OF COMPARATIVE LEGAL STUDY:
UEL's Experience

Nguyen Ngoc Dien   41

1. Interest of Comparative Law Study
2. Challenges and Solution
3. Illustration: UEL—Paris 2 Exchange Programme
4. Experience

Chapter 3:   INTERNATIONAL EXCHANGE PROGRAM(S) FOR LEGAL
EDUCATION AT THE FACULTY OF LAW AND PUBLIC
AFFAIRS OF PAÑÑĀSĀSTRA UNIVERSITY OF CAMBODIA

Kong Phallack and Phin Sovath   47

1. Introduction to Paññāsāstra University of Cambodia and the Faculty of
Law and Public Affairs
2. Why an International Exchange Program?
3. Outputs and Outcomes
4. Good Practice
5. Challenges of International Exchange Programs
6. Conclusions

Chapter 4:   THE CHALLENGES TO STUDY LAW ABROAD:
The International Cooperation and Exchange Program for
Legal Education at The Faculty of Law and Political science,
National University of Laos

Viengvilay Thiengchanhxay and Sonenaly Nanthavong   59

1. Introduction
2. International Cooperation and Exchange Program at FLP, NUOL
3. Outputs, Outcomes and Challenges
4. Conclusion

Chapter 5:   INTERNATIONAL EXCHANGE PROGRAMS AND
COLLABORATIONS FOR LEGAL EDUCATION
AT THAMMASAT UNIVERSITY

Junavit Chalidabhongse and Viravat Chantachote   69

1. Introduction
2. Overview of Law Programs Taught in Thai Language at Thammasat

CONTENTS

University Faculty of Law
3. Barriers Causing Problems to Students in Thai-taught LL.B. Program to Participate in an Exchange or Collaborative Program
4. New Development to Increase the Incentives for Students in Thai-taught LL.B. Program on Participating in an Exchange or Collaborative Program
5. Overview of Law Programs Taught in English Language at Thammasat University Faculty of Law
6. The Exchange Programs and Collaborations in English-taught Programs at Thammasat University Faculty of Law
7. Conclusion

Chapter 6: INTERNATIONAL STUDENT EXCHANGE PROGRAMS FOR LEGAL EDUCATION AT UNIVERSITY OF YANGON
Khin Chit Chit   83

1. Introduction
2. History of University of Yangon
3. Vision for the University of Yangon
4. Legal Education in University of Yangon
5. Requirement for Improvement of Legal Education
6. International Collaboration and Development Partners
7. Current Students at Law Department (2016-2017) Academic Year
8. International Student Exchange Programs
9. Benefits of International Student Exchange Programs
10. Challenges to International Student Exchange Programs
11. Conclusion

Chapter 7: COMPARATIVE LEGAL EDUCATION:
Challenges for Studying Law Abroad
Khin Phone Myint Kyu   93

1. Introduction
2. Facts about the University of Yangon
3. Human Resource Development Program (HRD) in University of Yangon
4. Regular Programs of Study at the University of Yangon
5. International Collaboration for Capacity Building
6. International Exchange Program for Legal Education
7. Problems and Obstacles for Further Development of International Exchange Programs
8. Conclusion

– vii –

Chapter 8:   GLOBALIZING JAPANESE LEGAL EDUCATION
AT KEIO UNIVERSITY LAW SCHOOL ("KLS"):
Exchange and Double Degree Arrangements as One Arrow
in the Quiver

David G. Litt   103

1. Introduction
2. The 2004 Legal Education Reform and the Japanese Law School System
3. Keio University Law School ("KLS") Programs
4. Out-bound Exchanges from Keio
5. Next Steps for KLS Globalization
6. Conclusion

COMMENTS

JAPANESE LAW TAUGHT IN ENGLISH

Susumu Masuda   121

1. My Presentation Topic
2. "Cross-Border Litigation" Course
3. My Teaching Methods
4. Difficulty (1) – Different Backgrounds
5. Difficulty (2) – English Materials for Japanese Laws
6. Difficulty (3) – Language
7. Conclusion

LOGISTICS FOR THE IMPLEMENTATION OF
INTERNATIONAL EXCHANGE PROGRAMS

Hitomi Fukasawa   127

1. Introduction
2. Start Living in Japan
3. Other Obstacles Abroad—The Language Barrier
4. Conclusion

PANEL DISCUSSION

How Can We Promote International Exchange Programs
for the Study of Law among Universities in the Asian Region?   137

CONTENTS

ON-SITE REPORTS

SPECIAL SUMMER PROGRAM ON COMPARATIVE AND INTERNATIONAL BUSINESS LAW SHORT REPORT

Mao Kimpav 161

FROM LAW CLASSROOMS IN ASIAN UNIVERSITIES:
Short Report on the Collaboration Program in Thailand

Hiroshi Matsuo and Hitomi Fukasawa 169

MATERIAL

COURSE CATALOGS

- Hanoi Law University, Vietnam 193
- University of Economics and Law, Vietnam National University, Hochiminh City 199
- Paññāsāstra University of Cambodia 206
- National University of Laos 216
- Thammasat University, Thailand 221
- University of Yangon, Myanmar 227
- Keio University Law School, Japan 235

INDEX 239

ABOUT KEIGLAD 241

ABOUT THE AUTHORS 242

INTRODUCTION

WHY IS IT WORTH CHALLENGING FOR STUDYING LAW ABROAD IN THE ASIAN REGION?

Hiroshi Matsuo*

(Keio University)

1. Advantages of Studying Law Abroad in the Asian Region

1.1 General Reasons to Study Law Abroad

It is widely recognized that legal education is strengthened by exchanging students and teachers between universities which have different advantageous resources. Each law school has its own international exchange programs with foreign partners. There are several reasons to study law in foreign universities. When I asked students who came from foreign countries or who experienced studying law overseas why they would like to study law abroad, the answers varied depending on their purposes and interests of doing so.[1] However, the reasons to study law

---

* This article is based on the introductory remarks of the Second Meeting on Comparative Legal Education in the Mekong Region Countries and Japan held on September 30, 2017 at Keio University Law School (for its details, see http://keiglad.keio.ac.jp/en/). I wish to gratefully acknowledge the participation of Mr. Kazumi Shindo, Director, Office for International Planning, Higher Education Policy Planning Division, Higher Education Bureau, Ministry of Education, Culture, Sports, Science and Technology.

[1] Parts of the answers are based on questionnaires distributed by the author in October 2017 at the law school classes of "Law and Development in East Asian Countries" and "Area Studies of Law (South East Asia)," to which around 40 students in total attended, who were orig-

abroad including those answers can be classified into the following categories.

(a) Acquiring In-Depth Knowledge of Foreign Law: First, it is advantageous for law students, law teachers, and legal professionals to understand foreign law by experiencing it in its natural context. They will discover not only the actual functions of formal law through practical applications to concrete cases but also the role of informal institutions that may coexist or supplement the formal institutions. They can learn foreign law in its own language, which will deepen the understanding of that law with the cultural background to be obtained from the insider's viewpoint close to the nationals. Thus, acquiring the in-depth knowledge of foreign law from Inside and its background is the major advantage of studying law abroad, which can be obtained only by living in that country and being deeply involved in its daily life. Additionally, deepening knowledge of the foreign legal system from its internal viewpoint may help students better understand the legal system of their home country, which is an important byproduct of studying law abroad.

(b) Conducting Comparative Legal Research: Second, interest in foreign law will naturally lead students to compare the form, content, and function of a particular law of the foreign legal system with that of their own country, to analyze the reasons for similarities as well as differences, to identify the common and special elements of that legal system, and thus enrich their knowledge of comparative law. Studying law abroad can be a rich source of comparative legal research, which seeks answers to fundamental questions about the functions, purposes, and essence of law. From this viewpoint, researchers can learn not only from teachers but also from classmates who come from different parts of the world. Students will become more open-minded and learn to approach fundamental questions about law from more flexible and broad perspectives.

(c) Learning Legal Theory: Third, they can learn the legal theory underlying the development of the foreign legal system where legal science has

---

inally from Italy, France, Portugal, Germany, Russia, the U.K., the U.S.A., Indonesia, South Korea, Brunei Darussalam, China, Vietnam, and Japan.

developed on the basis of a long history of legal research activities. The typical examples of these activities can be found in the historical accumulation of legal doctrines that have produced the legal systems known as Roman law, civil law, and common law. As a result, the mainstream of studying law abroad is made up of law students who went to prominent universities in Italy, and then students who went from developing countries to France, Germany, the U.K., and the U.S. This flow of theoretical knowledge of law is one of the main sources of "reception of law". Students can learn general principles of law, refined techniques of interpretation of law, and advanced methods of creating detailed provisions of law based on the long tradition of legal science. In this context, students who study law abroad have flowed mainly from non-Western countries to Western Countries, and from civil law countries to common law countries and vice versa.

(d) Learning Legal Practice: Fourth, legal practitioners who have business relationships with entities from a particular country go to that country to learn the practical treatment of actual legal cases. They can learn not only from legal experts in large cities, such as lawyers in big law firms, but also from local experts and create business networks with them. Furthermore, in the promotion of a globalized economy and the formation of standard international transaction rules by economic superpowers, law students and lawyers want to study law and practice in the countries that are producing those international standards. In this context, they have been going to the U.K., the U.S., and other English-speaking countries where they have opportunities to learn those common standards. They may also be qualified as lawyers of that country if they meet the requirements, such as obtaining an LL.M. degree and passing a bar examination in the U.S.

(e) Studying Law and Development and Finding the Spirit of Law: Finally, studying law abroad may bring some more benefits. It will expand the perspectives of students, teachers, and practitioners toward law because they will see the variety of law in different circumstances and stages of development. It may even change the observers' conception of law from a system of established rules to a system of transforming rules in accordance with the development process of a country. They will find that laws are not static and absolute rules, but dynamically changing rules relative to the circumstances of a society. This is the very concept of "spirit of laws" as Montesquieu tried to describe.[2] This dynamic and relative conception of law can be acquired more evidently in Asian countries where law has been used instrumentally to facilitate economic and political development which are indispensable parts of sustainable development goals. This conception of law is indispensable to identify the role of law for establishing good governance of each country which is a precondition for global governance as a collective body of countries that are achieving good governance without establishing a world government. In this context, the study of dynamic and relative features of law within the globally interconnected relationships will be a prerequisite for the globalization of legal education.

1.2　Special Advantages to Study Law in Asian Countries

In addition to the general advantages of studying law abroad as stated above, studying Asian legal systems in Asian countries has various advantages. They include increasing knowledge about the uniqueness of Asian laws within their cultural backgrounds, extending the horizon of comparative law, deepening understanding of legal theory by incorporating unique concepts of law and justice into the general theory of law, becoming familiar with the legal practices of emerging Asian markets, and identifying the role of law in the development process of Asian economies and political systems, which are unavoidably involved in the globalized system.

Various types of legal systems coexist in the Asian region.[3] The legal systems

---

[2] Montesquieu recognized that "the political and civil laws of each nation ought to be only the particular cases in which human reason is applied. … They should be in relation to the nature and principle of each government; … They should be in relation to the climate of each country; …". Charles Louis de Secondat Baron de la Brède et de Montesquieu, *DE L'ESPRIT DES LOIS*, Tome Premier, 1748, à Genève, Chez Barrillot & Fils, Partie I, Livre 1, Chapitre (3), Ligaran, 2014, p. 132.

[3] Poh-Ling Tan (ed.), *Asian Legal Systems: Law, Society and Pluralism in East Asia*, Butterworth, 1997.

of Malaysia, Singapore, Hong Kong Special Administrative Region (SAR), India, Pakistan, Bangladesh, and Sri Lanka have been influenced by common law through colonization by the U.K., while those of Japan, Korea, Taiwan, Thailand, and Cambodia have been influenced by civil law through the reception of law from France and Germany since the end of the 19th century. The legal systems of Indonesia and the Philippines have also been framed by civil law through Dutch and Spanish law. China, Vietnam, and Laos have adopted the socialist legal system that was amended by the introduction of market mechanisms since the middle of the 1980s. Islamic law is also widespread in Asian countries, such as in Malaysia, Indonesia, Pakistan, and Bangladesh. Thus, most of the major legal systems can be found in Asia.

(a) Studying law in Asian countries opens the door to diverse legal systems: It will increase the knowledge of each country's legal system in its unique language and within its cultural traditions and customs.

(b) Studying law in Asian countries will also expand the perspectives of comparative law: It will provide opportunities to compare the development of common law, civil law, socialist law and Islamic law which are adopted through the unique reception of law in Asian countries. Even among the common law countries in this region some differences and unique characteristics can be found in the legal system of Malaysia, Singapore, Hong Kong SAR, India, and Sri Lanka. The same applies to the civil law countries of Japan, Korea, Taiwan, Thailand, Cambodia, Indonesia, and the Philippines, and to the socialist law group of China, Vietnam, and Laos. The Islamic legal system is not identical in Malaysia, Indonesia, Pakistan, and Bangladesh. The comparative analysis between the different legal systems and within the same legal system in Asian countries will deepen the comparative perspectives of each major legal system.

(c) The concept of law in Asia has maintained a close relationship with the moral and religious precepts of Confucianism, Legalism, Hinduism, Buddhism, and Islam:[4] For instance, a code of conduct developed from Confu-

---

[4] Even within Buddhism, the code of conduct is different between Theravada Buddhism

cian and Legalist thought that originated in China and was transmitted to Korea and Japan has been profoundly connected with the concept of law in East Asian countries. This indicates that the standard theory of law fostered by Western legal thought could be further developed by including the unique concepts that have been intertwined with legal systems in Asian countries.[5] The same could be said about the concept of justice as a fundamental value of law. There was a hot debate on the Asian values which recognized the policy implementation by authoritarian government which was based on the significance of collective justice in Asian countries.[6] Thus, studying Asian law will contribute to the development of the theory of law and justice.

(d) **Learning the legal practices and the means of dispute resolution in Asian countries has important practical implications to facilitate international transactions:** There is an emerging center of growth in Asia, especially in the Mekong region countries, such as Vietnam, Laos, Cambodia, Thailand, and Myanmar. The establishment of the ASEAN Economic Community (AEC) in 2015 has further increased the practical importance to study law in ASEAN countries.

(e) **The economic growth in Asian countries highlights the relationship between legal reform and economic and political development:** A series of legal reforms, such as in property law, land law, contract law, tort law, law of secured transactions, company law, investment law, and civil procedure law, has played a positive role in economic development, particularly in the Mekong

---

widespread in Thailand, Cambodia, and Laos, on the one hand, and Mahayana Buddhism widespread in Vietnam, China, Hong Kong SAR, Taiwan, Korea, and Japan, on the other.

[5] The reconsideration of the concept of law will inevitably influence the understanding of "the rule of law" advocated as a common goal of legal development. See Hiroshi Matsuo, "Let the Rule of Law Be Flexible to Attain Good Governance," in: Per Bergling, Jenny Ederlöf and Veronica L. Taylor (eds.), *Rule of Law Promotion: Global Perspectives, Local Applications*, Iustus, Uppsala, pp. 41-56.

[6] As for the critical comment to the Asian values, see Amartya Sen, "Thinking About Human Rights and Asian Values," *Human Rights Dialogue*, 1.4, 1996; id., "Human Rights and Asian Values," *The New Republic*, July 14 & 21, 1997, pp. 33-40.

region countries. These countries provide us with rich materials for the study of law and development. We may find some patterns of virtuous cycles and negative cycles between political structure, legal reform, and economic development. Some Asian countries seem to show that the formation of strong government through the centralization of political powers was authorized by the constitutional reform; then the strengthened government undertook a series of legal reform programs for economic growth which were followed by another legal reform for equitable distribution; and thus the economic outcome led to the supportive participation by the citizen to the political decision making which promoted democracy with political stability.[7] Studying these patterns in Asian countries will allow observers to see law as a viable instrument to achieve economic growth with equity and political progress with stability and thus to establish good governance in a country, which can lead to the establishment of global governance as networks of countries with good governance. Studying the various challenges for legal reform experienced by Asian countries will provide opportunities for students who will contribute to the gradual formation of a system of global governance. Teachers in different countries can accumulate, exchange, and share materials on this subject in the Asian region, and they will become indispensable resources to explore the spirit of laws and to promote the globalization of legal education. Thus, when law is studied in Asian countries from the perspective of law and development, it has great significance.

2. Challenges for Studying Law Abroad in Asian Universities

2.1 Degree Programs

To realize the advantages discussed above by facilitating the mutual exchange of students and teachers among different universities in the Asian region,

---

[7] As for the sample analysis of Japan, see Ikuo Kabashima, "Supportive Participation with Economic Growth: The Case of Japan," *World Politics*, Vol. 36, 1984, pp. 332-338.

some problems need to be overcome through the cooperation. Some universities in Asia have opened degree programs, such as LL.B., LL.M., Ph.D., and J.D. programs, to foreign students. If those programs are provided in English, they are more accessible to foreign students. However, these programs, especially LL.B. and J.D. programs, are generally taught in the national language of the country in which the university is located, except for programs at universities such as in Singapore and Hong Kong, which are generally provided in English. This means that foreign candidates must learn that national language (a foreign language for the foreign students) to pass entrance examinations and to pursue many of these programs.

National languages are worth learning for students and researchers to understand the characteristics of the legal systems of foreign countries deeply, but it takes time for foreigners to master the foreign language enough to take the same course as the national students. To reduce this language gap, some universities provide degree programs, such as LL.M. and Ph.D. programs, in English. However, problems remain, including the limited number of students who can secure the time and money necessary to complete these degree programs.

Keio University Law School (hereinafter abbreviated KLS) launched its LL.M. program in April 2017, in which all the courses are taught in English.[8] As of now, around thirty students who passed the entrance examination, which is conducted twice a year by document review, have enrolled and studied in this program.[9] Students who want to learn Japanese have the opportunity to take Japanese classes provided by the Center for Japanese Studies.[10]

A program to acquire two degrees related to law, which is called "Double Degree program", may also be fruitful to realizing the advantages of studying law abroad in Asian countries. KLS has a formal Double Degree arrangement with the University of Washington School of Law in Seattle, U.S.A. (hereafter

---

[8] See the Course Catalogues at the end of this volume.

[9] For the basic information on the KLS-LL.M. Program, see < http://www.ls.keio.ac.jp/en/llm/>.

[10] For the Japanese courses, see <http://www.cjs.keio.ac.jp/?page=&lang=en>.

abbreviated as UWL),[11] under which students will be able to obtain LL.M. degrees from both schools. A student will pay KLS tuition fees during their time at Keio and UWL tuition fees during their time at UWL. A typical KLS student might enroll at KLS for the spring term from April through July, and then study at UWL from September through March (Autumn and Winter quarters), and then enroll again at KLS for the spring term after returning from UWL. The Double Degree program at UWL may allow some students to qualify to sit for a U.S. state bar examination, although the details will vary by individual depending on education content, timing of the degree, and practical experience.[12]

Other Double Degree programs may be added. In the future, if a mutual agreement for the dual degree program is concluded, for instance, between KLS and Hanoi Law University in Vietnam (hereinafter abbreviated as HLU), a student who enrolled in the program could take KLS courses in the first semester, which starts in April and ends in July, then move to the LL.M. course at HLU and take courses for one year, from August through next June, to study Vietnamese laws and development, and then return to KLS to complete the final semester from September to March of the next year. The candidate may be able to finish all the courses within two years and obtain Master's Degrees in Law from HLU and KLS. This aims to serve as an academic passport for graduates who would like to work in the globalizing Asian market or apply for employment in international organizations.

2.2 Non-Degree Programs

Non-degree programs provided in English and for shorter terms with smaller fees can be flexibly arranged for foreign students and researchers who want to study foreign law. The terms may be 6 months (one semester), 3 months, 1

---

[11] UWL currently offers LL.M. degrees in categories such as Asian & Comparative Law, Global Business, Health Law, Intellectual Property, Sustainable International Development, Tax, and General Law. See <https://www.law.uw.edu/academics/llm/>.

[12] For more details, see <http://www.ls.keio.ac.jp/en/Double%20Degree%20Fact%20 Sheet%20and%20Schedule%2020171227.pdf>.

month, or 2 weeks in accordance with the purpose and content of the program. In these programs, topic-oriented courses may be arranged to meet the needs of students and researchers. Credits may be awarded to students who meet the requirements of the host university.

These programs may be jointly provided by participant universities which share the common interest in the challenge of providing them. As an example of one of these programs, KLS has conducted joint programs as part of the Program for Asian Global Legal Professions (PAGLEP). In March 2017, KLS carried out externship programs in collaboration with the Vietnam National University of Economics and Law in Ho Chi Minh (hereinafter abbreviated as UEL) and Pannasastra University of Cambodia Faculty of Law and Public Affairs (hereinafter abbreviated as PUC-FLPA). In the UEL/KLS externship program, Japanese J.D. students visited UEL and participated in special lectures on current legal issues in Vietnamese law[13] and Japanese law[14] with Vietnamese students at UEL. They also made joint presentations on a solution for a common issue by applying Vietnamese law and Japanese law and discussed the similarities and differences of the solutions and their reasons.[15] In the PUC-FLPA/KLS externship program, Japanese J.D. students and Cambodian students took special lectures on current legal issues in Cambodian law[16] and Japanese law[17] at PUC-FLPA. Then, they made presentations and had discussions similar to those at UEL.[18] In September 2017, a similar externship program was conducted by KLS at Tammasat Uni-

---

[13] On the Vietnamese laws of international trade.

[14] On the Japanese case laws of mergers and acquisitions, and those of tort liability of supervisors of a person who has a limited mental capacity.

[15] See Hiroshi Matsuo and Hitomi Fukasawa, "From Law Classrooms in Asian Universities: Short Report on the Collaboration Program in Vietnam and Cambodia," in: KEIGLAD (ed.), *Comparative Legal Education from Asian Perspective, Program for Asian Global Legal Professions Series I*, Keio University Press, 2017, pp. 157-164.

[16] On the Cambodian law and practice of intellectual property.

[17] On the Japanese case laws of mergers and acquisitions, and those of tort liability of supervisors for a person who has a limited mental capacity (the same as provided at UEL).

[18] See Matsuo and Fukasawa (note 15 above), pp. 164-167.

versity in Thailand (hereinafter abbreviated as TUL), which consisted of special lectures on current issues in Thai law and Japanese law, class observations, and students' presentations on a common issue.

In August 2017, KLS also organized and conducted the PAGLEP Summer Seminar, in which LL.M. students and lecturers from HLU, UEL, PUC-FLPA, TUL, National University of Laos Faculty of Law and Political Science (hereinafter abbreviated as NUOL-FLP), and Yangon University Faculty of Law (hereinafter abbreviated as YUL) participated with KLS J.D. and LL.M. students. This program included lectures on International Trade Law and WTO Law, Current Issues in Japanese Law (public law and private law), Court Observation,[19] a Workshop on International Trade, and Presentations on Common Topic.[20]

The Externship Programs and the Summer Seminar Program mentioned above were conducted as trials to discover the benefits and challenges of joint programs established through collaborations among Asian universities. We have found that the focus of legal education and its pedagogical method depends on the social needs for and basic conditions of legal education, which are influenced by economic and political circumstances. Therefore, we can talk about neither the best teaching methods nor the best learning styles apart from the specific contexts of each country's development situation. At the same time, we have also confirmed that there is ample room to improve the pedagogical method of legal education by exchanging ideas through collaboration programs, which will also influence the function of legal system and the conditions for economic and political development. However, we still face problems in the promotion of collaboration programs.

---

[19] Court Observation was conducted at Yokohama District Court. I thank Mr. Shigeyuki Fukasawa, Judge at Yokohama District Court, for his special lecture and favors provided during our visit.

[20] The Common Topic was concerning the solution of the conflict due to impossibility of performance of contractual obligation.

3. Obstacles to Studying Law Abroad in the Asian Region

3.1 Differences in Legal Education Systems

Even though more trials of collaboration programs are being conducted, we face various problems to improve the international exchange programs further. The most serious obstacles experienced by exchange students include differences in legal education systems, language barriers, obtaining scholarships, and securing affordable accommodations. We need to examine candidly these problems from the perspective of students, teachers, and administrative staff respectively to clarify the reality of these problems.

The obstacles concerning legal education systems include the differences in required standards for admission, curricula, semester terms in university calendar, teaching methods, studying styles, grading systems, and requirements for obtaining degree. These differences may sometimes cause foreign students to become overwhelmed.

The difference in the duration and the start and the end of semesters may create gaps between the end of a term at the home university and the start of the term at a foreign university.[21] The semester terms are fixed traditionally in each country, influenced by the fiscal year of government organizations and companies, and will be difficult to unify.

The differences in assessment between the grading systems may also be a problem. For example, KLS adopts the grading style such that an "S" grade with 4.0 grade points is given to the top 15% of students in each class, an "A" with 3.0 grade points is given to the next 25%, a "B" with 2.0 grade points is given to the next 40%, and a "C" with 1.0 grade points is given to the next 20%, and a "D" is given to the students who fail the class. Students who obtain an S, A, B, or C pass the class and are given credit points (different from grade points) depending the content and duration of the class. If a class is 15-week course with 90 minutes

---

[21] See "Material: Duration of the Semester," in: KEIGLAD (ed.), op. cit. (note 11 above), pp. 176-177.

WHY IS IT WORTH CHALLENGING FOR STUDYING LAW ABROAD IN THE ASIAN REGION?

per week, a student is given 2 credit points for passing the class. If it is an 8-week course with 90 minutes per week, a student is given 1 credit point for passing the class.[22] Credit points are given to students who pass the class in accordance with the number of 90-minute units. To graduate, the J.D. students need to obtain no less than 100 credit points (69 credit points for compulsory subjects and more than 31 credit points from elective subjects) and a no less than 1.5 grade point average (GPA). For the LL.M. students, no less than 36 credit points and a no less than 1.5 GPA is necessary to complete the course. However, the assessment method for grading differs from university to university even within the Asian region. In some universities, the evaluation method seems to be more structured and objectively opened to students in advance than others. The difference in the grade point system and the credit point system may disturb the transfer of credit points from one university to another, and the recognition of grade points issued by one university may not be equally evaluated by another university.[23]

To promote the exchange of students and to provide them with tuition fees exemption and recognition of credit points transfer, it usually is necessary for universities to conclude a Memorandum of Agreement for Mutual Exchange and Cooperation (hereafter abbreviated as MOA). However, the procedure and the requirements for MOAs differ widely among universities. In some universities,

---

[22] Some classes may be held twice or more in one week intensively, and in this case the credit points are given in accordance with the number of 90-minute units. For externship programs with the duration of more than 8 days, 1 credit point may be given to students who complete them.
[23] For the further promotion of the international transfer of credit points, the Ministry of Education, Culture, Sports, Science and Technology in Japan drafted "ASEAN Plus Three Guidelines on Transcripts and Supplemental Documents for Academic Record of Exchange Students" (as of October 27, 2017). It includes the recommended information and description of transcripts and supplemental documents, the conversion table for the credit transfer system between Asian Credit Transfer System by ASEAN University Network [AUN-ACTS], University Mobility in Asia and the Pacific Credit Transfer [UCTS], European Credit Transfer System [ECTS], Latin American Reference Credit [CLAR], Credit for Accumulation and Transfer Scheme [CATS] by the U.K. system, and credit transfer by the U.S.A. system, and the sample of transcript for exchange student. See <http://www.mext.go.jp/en/policy/education/highered/title02/detail02/sdetail02/sdetail02/1383529.htm>.

the negotiation is conducted and the decision made by the corresponding faculty, law school, or university, while in other universities the government's approval is necessary in addition to the agreement between the partner universities, and it is sometimes hard to predicate when the government permission will be granted. Without concluding an MOA, the cooperating universities cannot mutually invite students, register exchange students as regular students, issue certificates for completion of courses, or recognize the transfer of credit points and the evaluation of grade points, and consequently, students will face difficulties acquiring visas.

3.2 Language Barriers

The language barrier is the biggest obstacle for students when they study abroad, particularly in Asian countries. In Asia, almost all countries have their own national languages, including Burmese, Thai, Lao, Khmer, Vietnamese, Malay, Indonesian, Tetum, Filipino, Sinhala, Tamil, Chinese, Korean, and Japanese. Only in Singapore, is English recognized as one of the national languages, together with Malay, Chinese, and Tamil. Not only the provisions of law, regulations, and court decisions, but also most of the textbooks and other materials are written in national languages. In those documents, many special terms are used. In universities, most programs are provided in the national language with few exceptions. The number of classes, programs, or courses on legal subjects taught in English are still small.[24] As a result, research materials, which are available for foreign students to use in their study of law, are very limited.

Additionally, when students begin to live in foreign country, they are often required to fill out various applications in that country's language to register themselves at the city office, open bank account, and have a certificate of eligibility issued. Important notices from government offices are usually written in the national language.

---

[24] For example, see Course Catalogues of the universities participating to the PAGLEP in MATERIAL at the end of this book.

3.3 Costs and Accommodations

It is costly to study law abroad, especially in big cities. Students must pay travel expenses, accommodation fees, tuition and registration fees to the university, in addition to insurance fees, and other expenses necessary to live in a foreign country.[25]

When a university concludes an MOA, which includes the mutual exemption of tuition fees with his/her home university, the student may be exempted from tuition fees if he/she pays them to his/her home university. However, this agreement is based on mutual exchange, so it will be conditioned on the proper balance of the number of inbound and outbound students.

In the case in which this agreement is not applied, students must pay tuition fees at the foreign university themselves. In this case, several types of scholarships are provided by government-funded organizations, NGOs, companies, and individuals, although the amount of funding for scholarship is still limited for students who want to study law abroad in Asia.

The difficulty in finding affordable accommodations can be an invisible impediment to studying abroad. Landlords may not want to lease their property to foreign tenants. In some big cities in Asia, it is not easy to find proper accommodations with reasonable rent for foreigners. There may be also customary rules to pay thanks money and security deposits other than a rent. Accommodation is a serious problem for foreign students, particularly those who need to stay longer to complete a degree program or take courses that continue for one semester or several months. There is some support for foreign students that is provided by universities. However, it is not always enough to secure affordable accommodations.

3.4 Inadequate Information

It is crucial for a foreign student who plans to study law abroad to have easy

---

[25] See Hitomi Fukasawa, "Logistics for the Implementation of International Exchange Programs," this volume, Section 2.1 and 2.2, pp. 128-132.

access to accurate and up-to-date information on the required qualifications, eligibility, and entrance examinations for the university to which he/she would like to attend, as well as of the concrete content and features of curricula, grading system, degree requirements, availability of exemption of fees, scholarship, accommodation, other possible costs for living in a language that every foreign student can easily understand. However, not all universities are responsive to these requests. Sometimes information is fragmented among different divisions of the university and is not always updated.[26]

4. Possible Measures to Eliminate Obstacles

4.1 Filling the Gaps in the Legal Education System

Differences in legal education systems, as indicated above (3.1), are not easily unified. Differences in semester terms in the university calendars are difficult to change because they are sometimes interrelated with other economic and political systems in the countries. However, gaps in semester terms may be utilized to prepare for the study abroad. For instance, if the university to which a foreign student wants to go to study law provides certain non-degree programs of, for instance, an introduction to the legal system of that country or a basic course of the national language of that country it could be useful for the student to complete those programs before the new semester starts in that foreign university. Thus, the usage of non-degree programs may flexibly cover the gaps due to the rigidity of semester terms.

Differences in eligibility requirements, curricula, grading systems, and degree requirements do not need to be unified, but there may be room to rearrange the curricula and grading system to transfer credit points and recognize grade points between universities. This would be greatly beneficial for students

---

[26] Sunaryati Hartono (ed.), *ASEAN Cooperation in Legal Education*, the National Law Development Agency, Jakarta, Indonesia, 1989, p. 18.

and will facilitate the future exchange of students who will study law in foreign universities. For instance, it would be worthwhile for law schools in the Asian region to study each other's curricula and grading systems, rearrange their curricula to adopt the strengths of each university, reasonably restructure the grading system, and negotiate collaborative programs in which academic credits transfer and foreign grades are recognized for students who want to become specialists of Asian legal systems.[27] If this adaptation is promoted, the differences in curricula will no longer be a problem, but will become attractive features of each university. In this sense, differences are important and unique characteristics of each law school and are the very reason that it is meaningful for foreign students to study abroad. These students will understand the old Asian saying that once one enters a village, they follow the rules of the village. However, kind guidance for foreign students to become familiar with the local system is important.

As for the differences in teaching methods and studying styles, teachers and students can learn about each other through mutual exchange programs. The trials of degree programs and non-degree programs for exchange students described above are also a part of the mutual learning experience among partner universities to improve teaching methods and studying styles further.[28]

4.2 Overcoming the Language Barrier

The language barrier is an obstacle as well as an advantage for students who study abroad. The challenge is changing the obstacle into an advantage. There may be two steps in this process.

First, it would be effective to increase the programs and the materials available in a popular language in Asia, such as English, which will guide foreign students to the national legal systems of a country dynamically developing through globalization.[29]

---

[27] The ASEAN University Network (AUN) will enhance mutual collaboration among universities in ASEAN, China, Korea, and Japan, see <http://www.aunsec.org/index.php>.

[28] See 2.1 and 2.2 above.

[29] Within the framework of the PAGLEP, the Meeting on the Common Material for Legal Ed-

Second, there seems to be an ample room to create programs and materials for students to learn the foreign language using legal materials, in which the basic terms and sentences in that foreign language can be translated into English. However, this is a long term project that can only be promoted step-by-step.

A tutoring system may also be effective in assisting foreign students in their daily lives. Tutors can be recruited from the host university. They can guide foreign students to government offices, bank, and other places, and provide consultation for both academic and non-academic matters.

4.3 Mitigating Cost and Accommodation Problems

The conclusion of an MOA, which includes the mutual exemption of tuition fees, is the first priority in mitigating the cost of studying abroad. Then, the sources of scholarships may be expanded from government organizations, international institutions, private foundations, and NGOs to include companies that have special relationships with the Asian region. Those private companies have a good reason to invest in the development of human resources who can take a leadership role in solving conflicts that occur in the globalizing Asian market.

As for accommodations, if there are not enough university dormitories for foreign students, then private apartment houses should be found that are available for foreign students. To secure lodging for foreign students, it is important for universities to maintain contact with landlords who can provide accommodation. It will enrich the information available for accommodation and relieve foreign students of the challenge in securing their accommodations before they move abroad.[30]

4.4 Facilitating Information Exchange and Smooth Communication

The up-to-date provision of precise information about eligibility require-

---

ucation is held on January 12 and 13, 2018 at KLS for this purpose.

[30] See Fukasawa, op. cit. (note 25), Section 2.1, pp. 128-131.

ments, curricula, grading systems, degree requirements, tuition fees, accommodations, and other costs as well as the advantageous benefits of studying law at each university is important for recruiting students. This information should not be fragmented among different sources, but concentrated in one site to provide a one-stop service for foreign students. It is also worth placing the tutors as consultation staffs for foreign students. The collaborating law schools may negotiate a common format for the provision of important information about the study of law for foreign students. The free flow of information and smooth communication with foreign law schools should lead to the construction of a common market for legal education where students can enjoy shopping for individual courses, a set of non-degree programs, or a degree program that fit their needs at a reasonable cost in order to improve their abilities as legal professionals in the globalizing Asian market.

5. Constructing a Common Market among Law Schools toward the Globalization of Legal Education

The construction of a common market for legal education in the Asian region is only the starting point for further development toward the globalization of legal education. However, what does the globalization of legal education mean? Will it mean to empower students to conduct business across borders and cultures? Will it mean to enable students to meet clients' needs to compete in globalized economy? Or, will it mean to help law schools become global centers for legal research and learning? Seeking for the true meaning of the globalization of legal education cannot stop there. The significance of facilitating students' opportunities to study law abroad in Asian law schools is not limited to the economic and regional aspects but may create more comprehensive structure to foster legal professionals who can take initiatives to realize the global interest.

The study of law abroad in the Asian region will provide students with the key to deeper fields of legal transactions where they will be able to play an active role in solving difficult issues—including business conflicts, international security issues, environmental issues, and human rights issues—not from the narrow scope of their national interest, but from a broader perspective that will contribute to the sustainable development of the world. It will lead to the globalization of legal education in its true sense.

For that purpose, however, the most important thing to do now is to make more attractive programs for domestic and foreign students through the continued exchange of students among collaborating law schools.

COUNTRY REPORTS

Chapter 1

THE IMPLEMENTATION OF STUDENT EXCHANGE PROGRAMS:

Some Issues from the Hanoi Law University Perspective

Nguyen Van Quang*

(Hanoi Law University)

1. The Context: Internationalisation and International Collaboration at Hanoi Law University

In the current globalisation context, internationalisation has become an apparent trend in the development strategies of many universities in the world.[1] Despite having some negative impacts, university internationalisation brings many benefits for the development of universities among which "more internationally oriented staff/students and improved academic quality" is of significant importance.[2] In such context, Vietnamese universities cannot go against the common

---

* Ph.D. Associate Professor of Law, Hanoi Law University, Vietnam. Many thanks to Anne Nguyen, a student of Barnard College, Columbia University, US for her English language editing. All errors remaining in this paper are mine.

[1] See Rui Yang, University internationalization: its meanings, rationales and implications, *Intercultural Education, Vol. 13, No.1, 2002,* pp 81-95, available at http://firgoa.usc.es/drupal/files/internationalisation.pdf (last accessed on November 25, 2017); Ross Hudson, *Why universities want to internationalise; what stops them,* available at https://www.britishcouncil.org/voices-magazine/why-universities-want-to-internationalise-what-stops-them (last accessed on November 25, 2017).

[2] See Jane Knight, Internationalisation brings important benefits as well as risks, *Interna-*

– 25 –

trend of internationalisation. The efforts of Vietnam to internationalise higher education have been reflected in several policies, projects and programs initiated by the Government, the Ministry of Education and Training (MOET), related Ministries and industries and other stakeholders.[3] It is evident that in Vietnam much investment has been put in several key elements of higher education institutions including faculty/staff members, students, curriculum/textbooks and academic quality assurance. In fact, to a certain extent, some Vietnamese universities have made impressive progresses towards university internationalisation.[4]

Obviously, international collaboration plays a key role in promoting university internationalisation. The more active in international collaboration a university is, the better opportunities it has towards its internationalisation goal. To evaluate how well a university conduct its international collaboration activities, in Vietnam, we normally take into consideration several criteria including: (i) the number of its international academic partners; (ii) the degree of participation of international faculty members in its teaching and research activities; (iii) the degree of participation of its faculty members in international teaching and research activities; (iv) the number of its students participating in international student exchange programs; and the number of international students studying at the university.

Given the above-mentioned criteria, the degree of being active in interna-

---

tional Higher Education, Vol 46, Winter 2007, available at https://ejournals.bc.edu/ojs/index.php/ihe/article/view/7939/7090 (last accessed on November 25, 2017).

[3] See Pham Hiep, *Quốc tế hóa giáo dục đại học ở Việt Nam, những nỗ lực từ trên xuống* [*Internationalising higher education in Vietnam – the top-down efforts*], available at http://giaoduc.net.vn/Giao-duc-24h/Quoc-te-hoa-giao-duc-dai-hoc-Viet-Nam-nhung-no-luc-tu-tren-xuong-post165489.gd (last accessed on November 25, 2017).

[4] They are the Vietnam National University (Ha Noi), the Vietnam National University (Ho Chi Minh City), FPT University, Duy Tan University and Ton Duc Thang University. For more details, see Pham Hiep, *Quốc tế hóa giáo dục đại học, nhìn từ các đại học hàng đầu Việt Nam* [*Internationalising higher education seen from the leading universities of Vietnam*], available at http://giaoduc.net.vn/Giao-duc-24h/Quoc-te-hoa-dai-hoc-nhin-tu-cac-dai-hoc-hang-dau-Viet-Nam-post165492.gd (last accessed on November 25, 2017).

THE IMPLEMENTATION OF STUDENT EXCHANGE PROGRAMS

tional collaboration of Vietnamese universities varies greatly, depending on specific circumstances and conditions of each university. This is also the case for Vietnamese law schools. While the more experienced law schools have actively designed and implemented various international collaboration programs, several limitations in this practice can be identified in the younger ones. Pursuing the goal of being one of the two key national law schools training legal human resource by 2020 with the great support of the Government of Vietnam,[5] Hanoi Law University has proved to be a pioneering Vietnamese law school in promoting international collaboration.

First, Hanoi Law University has successfully completed a number of collaboration projects funded by international donors, greatly contributing to the infrastructure development and the enhancement of its academic and management capabilities. Notable examples of those projects include: (i) "Retraining Legal Officials for the Government of Vietnam", funded by Asia Development Bank (ADB) (from 1998 to 2001)[6]; (ii) "Strengthening Legal Education in Vietnam" sponsored by the Swedish Government through the Swedish International Development Cooperation Agency (SIDA) (from 1998 to 2012)[7]; and (iii)"Strenthening Capacity in International Trade Law through Training and Research for Universities, Government Agencies, Legal Practitioners and Businesses in Vietnam" with EU as the sponsor and EU-VIETNAM MUTRAP III (Vietnam's Ministry

---

[5] See Decision 549/QĐ-TTg of Prime Minister of Vietnam dated on April 4th, 2013 on approval of the Comprehensive Project on Promoting Hanoi Law University and Ho Chi Minh City University of Law as Key Law Schools Training Legal Human Resource.

[6] Under this Project over 1000 legal officials were re-trained by Hanoi Law University's teaching staff by the end of 2001. Thanks to the Project, not only the practice skills of the legal officials were improved, but the academic capacity of Hanoi Law University's teaching staff was also much enhanced.

[7] The Project mainly aimed at improving the curriculum and teaching methods of Hanoi Law University to be corresponding with legal education in the rule of law context, enhancing law training and research capabilities by improving staff's professional competencies and reinforcing the information and library system of the University.

of Industry and Trade) as the governing body (from 2009 to 2012).[8]

Second, Hanoi Law University has paid close attention to fostering partnerships with many top-notch law schools in Asia, Oceania, Europe and North America.[9] The University makes considerable efforts to implement the partnership agreements under a range of specific activities such as co-organising conferences/workshops, co-conducting research, joint teaching programs, student and staff mobility and exchange of academic materials and publications. Such international collaboration activities have brought many positive impacts on the capacity building of Hanoi Law University towards the goal of university internationalisation.

Third, Hanoi Law University, as one of the very few law schools of Vietnam, has in its structure the foreign law reseach and education centres supported by the international donors and the University itself. Nagoya University Reseach and Education Centre for Japanese Law operated under the support of the Government of Japan and the Government of Vietnam has smoothly run on the campus of Hanoi Law University since 2007. Coures in Japanese language and Japanese law are taught by several lecturers from Nagoya University who work full-time at Hanoi Law University. Similarly, thanks to the support of some German institutions such as Friedrich Ebert Stiftung (FES) and German Academic Exchange Service (DAAD) and some other German Universities, German Law Centre at Hanoi Law Univesity was established in 2010. In the Centre, some German professors together with their Vietnamese colleagues currently teach German language, German and European law in English and German and conduct research works.

Fourth, Hanoi Law University has recently reformed its curriculum, meeting

---

[8] Thanks to this Project, much improvement in curriculum development, teaching methods, textbook development and research works regarding international trade law has been evidenced at Hanoi Law University.

[9] Currently, Hanoi Law University collaborates with about 30 foreign law school partners. The list of current partner law schools of Hanoi Law University is available at http://hlu.edu. vn/News/Details/16490 (last accessed on November 25, 2017). See Appendix 1 of this paper for further details.

the context of international integration. Upon the reform, besides the substantive content, the critical inclusion of several courses taught in English into the curriculum is also worth noting.[10] A new LLB in international trade and business law under which some courses are taught in English by foreign guest lecturers and the teaching staff of Hanoi Law University has been offered since 2012.[11] The University also designs a special program attracting "high quality" students and it is expected that 20% of the program courses are taught in English by the faculty of Hanoi Law University. Besides law programs, Hanoi Law University is beginning to diversify its curriculum by adding a BA in English language with legal English specialty to its curriculum. More interestingly, a short course titled "Introduction to the Vietnamese Legal System" taught in English by Hanoi Law University's lecturers for international students has been introduced. The course offers a brief introduction to the main areas of Vietnamse laws together with opportunities to observe real procedures of Vietnamese local courts or law firms, attracting more and more international students.[12]

Undeniably, Hanoi Law University has made great efforts to promote international collaboration towards to the goal of university internationalisation. The question of how far the international collaboration activities of Hanoi Law University have been effectively running, however, still remains. In particular, given the fact that the number of foreign partners of Hanoi Law University has been increasing, whether its student exchange programs are well implemented. Section 2 below closely examines the current practice of student exchange programs at Hanoi Law University and explains why the University needs to put further

---

[10] For LLB curriculum of Hanoi Law University, see http://hlu.edu.vn/News/Details/16483 (last accessed on November 25, 2017).

[11] For LLB in international trade law curriculum of Hanoi Law University, see http://pltmqt. hlu.edu.vn/Images/Post/files/Khoa%20PLTMQT/Curriculum-Major%20in%20ITBL-HLU-Sep%202011-English.pdf (last accessed on November 25, 2017).

[12] For examples, in 2016, 07 students of the University of San Francisco (US), 05 students of the University of New Castle (Australia) and 10 students of Waikato University (New Zealand) came to take this course at Hanoi Law University; in 2017, 04 students of the University of San Francisco (US) and 10 students of Waikato University attended the course.

– 29 –

efforts into the implementation of these programs.

2. Student Exchange Programs at Hanoi Law University: the Fact

In the context of higher education, a student exchange program normally refers to one under which students from a home university go to study at a host university for a semester (or a full academic year) without paying tution fees to the host university and all credits accumulated by the home students at the host university are recognised by the home university. Much has been discussed about the benefits of student exchange programs in general and this paper does not intend to repeat them.[13] Among about 30 current foreign law school partners of Hanoi Law University, those which are active in student exchange programs are very few and the number of students of these programs is still modest.[14] Below are some examples.

The Faculty of Law at the National University of Singapore is the first partner law school with whom Hanoi Law University has had a student exchange program. Since 2008, the Faculty of Law at the National University of Singapore has annually received 1 student from Hanoi Law University for the one-semester exchange program. Hanoi Law University, however, has not yet received any students from the National University of Singapore for such programs. Similarly, the National University of Taiwan is an active partner of student exchange with Hanoi Law University and since 2012 it has annually received 2 or 3 students from Hanoi Law University for the one-sesmeter exchange program. In the case

---

[13] For a brief discussion of the benefits of student exchange programs, see for example, *The outcomes of outbound student mobility* available at http://aimoverseas.com.au/wp-content/uploads/2013/08/UAAsiaBoundOutcomesResearch-Final.pdf (last accessed on November 25, 2017).

[14] The statistical data shown in this section are extracted from the Reports of the International Cooperation of Hanoi Law University (those Reports are on file with the author). See Appendix 2 and Appendix 3 of this paper for further details.

of Nagoya University in Japan, thanks to the support of the Ministry of Education, Culture, Sports, Science and Technology (MEXT) of Japan, from 2013 to 2017, 3 students from Hanoi Law University went to Nagoya University for the one-sesmeter exchange program and Hanoi Law University also received 2 students from Nagoya University for the similar study program. Especially, Akron Law School (Ohio, United States of America) is the first American partner with whom Hanoi Law University has launched the one-sesmester student exchange program and 2 students of Hanoi Law University were sent to Akron Law Schoon in 2017.

Besides one-semester exchange programs, based on bilateral agreements, Hanoi Law University and its partners also exchange students on a short-term basis ranging from one to four weeks. Under the agreement between Hanoi Law University and Nagoya University, from 2013 to 2017, Nagoya University sent 10 students to Hanoi Law University for a one-week exchange program and Nagoya University also received 6 students from Hanoi Law University for a three-week exchange program. In collaboration with the University of Applied Sciences (HTW), Berlin, Germany, Hanoi Law University applies a different form of student exchange thanks to the support of German sponsors (Friedrich Ebert Stiftung - FES and German Academic Exchange Service -DAAD). Since 2012, HTW and Hanoi Law University have annually organised a 10-day summer or sping school in Vietnam for about 20 students of both Universities. These summer or spring schools, entirely taught in English by German and Vietnamese professors, focus on specific topics relating to human rights and civil rights.

In comparision with other law schools in Vietnam, what Hanoi Law University has done for its student exchange programs is worth being commendable. However, given the fact that Hanoi Law University has a significant number of foreign university partners, the limitations of its student exchange programs have become the common concern of many people. There are several reasons why the implementation of student exchange programs at Hanoi Law University is still limited.

First, it is noted that student exchange programs, by nature, are mutually beneficial to the home and host universities. This means that once student exchange programs are launched, partner universities always try their best to balance inbound and outbound students. In the case of Hanoi Law University, while the number of outbound students has been increasing, it is expected that Hanoi Law University should have more inbound students. This practice is largely due to the University's limited capacity to deliver courses taught in English. Although Hanoi Law University has made significant efforts to design courses taught in English, international students have only limited opportunities to choose relevant courses for their exchange programs at Hanoi Law University. In the current LLB curriculum of Hanoi Law University, only 10 elective modules taught in English are offered.[15] The situation is even worse for post-graduate students as no courses taught in English are availabe in LLM and PhD programs at Hanoi Law University. In addition, due to the lack of resources, the modules taught in English are not always available throughout the academic year. Above all, Hanoi Law University faces many difficulties in developing and teaching courses in English. For lecturers whose English is not their first language or who have not experienced studying abroad with English as the language of instruction, teaching an entire course in English is not an easy task. Unfortunately, the majority of lecturers of Hanoi Law University falls within the above-mentioned category.[16] In addition, Hanoi Law University is not really active in faculty exchange programs due to costs and logistics barriers and thus its lecturers do not have many opportunities to share their experiences teaching courses in English with their international colleagues. This practice, associated with the lack of materials especially those relating to Vietnamese law available in English, makes teaching coures in English at Hanoi Law University more challenging.

Second, the barrier of financial difficulties also causes some problems for

---

[15] See the current LLB curriculum of Hanoi Law University at http://hlu.edu.vn/News/Details/16483 (last accessed on November 25, 2017) for some details of 10 modules taught in English which are currently offered in the LLB program at Hanoi Law University.

[16] Statistically, there are about 20 lecturers (out of more than 300 lecturers) of Hanoi Law University who are able to give lectures in English on certain subject matters.

implementing student exchange programs at Hanoi Law University. Although most partner universities generously exempt tuition and fees for students of Hanoi Law University under the student exchange programs, expensive travel fares and high living costs in delevopled countries like Australia, Singapore, Japan or United States cannot be easily overcome. This is quite understandable considering Vietnam is one of the lower middle-income countries. In practice, cases where students who qualify for student exchange but cannot afford the expenses so they have to withdraw from the program are not rare at Hanoi Law University.[17]

Third, studying one or two sesmesters in foreign law schools, especially in countries whose legal tradition is different from that of Vietnam, is quite challenging for many students of Hanoi Law University. Not only does the English language, but also the study load and the differences in learning, teaching and research cultures cause several problems for students of Hanoi Law University in student exchange programs. For instance, in a recent interview with some students who experienced a semester at the Faculty of Law of the National University of Singapore, the following difficulties that Hanoi Law University's students faced were drawn: (i) English as the language of instruction; (ii) heavy study load, especially the reading requirements; (iii) studying case law; (iv) active participation in class; and (v) criteria for assessment, especially for writing tasks. While we expect that students of Hanoi Law University should learn to deal with these difficulties, to a certain exent, they also discourage students of Hanoi Law University from participating in student exchange programs.

Fourth, apart from the limitations above, the differences in semester dates among partner universities may also negatively affect the decision to join stu-

---

[17] On average, a student in Vietnam spends about VND 2,500,000 – 3,000,000 (roughly USD 100 – 120) per month for food, accommodation, travel and miscellaneous items which is far below the living cost in developed countries such as UK, US, Australia and Germany (see: *Chi phí của sinh viên đại học* [*Expenses for university students*] available at https:// thanhnien.vn/giao-duc/chi-phi-cua-mot-sinh-vien-hoc-dai-hoc-191658.html (last accessed at November 25, 2017).

dent exchange programs of students of Hanoi Law University. In some cases, if students decide to participate in a one-semester student exchange program, they normally would miss the next semester at their home university after coming back from the host university due the differences mentioned above. For instance, while semester one of Hanoi Law University starts in the middle of August, Nagoya University in Japan begins its sesmeter one in early October.[18] The exchange students of Hanoi Law University at Nagoya University usually finish their semester one in March when their semester two at Hanoi Law University has been running for at least two months. As a result, students who enroll in student exchange programs with Nagoya University normally complete their programs at Hanoi Law University few months behind the scheduled time.

The above analysis has clearly shown that the implementation of student exchange programs at Hanoi Law University needs several improvements for the purposes of university internationalisation. The question of how student exchange programs at Hanoi Law University should be improved and promoted becomes more critical in the context that significant achievements have been made towards the process of regional integration in the ASEAN countries. Section 3 below offers some suggestions of how to promote student exchange programs at Hanoi Law University given the current context of ASEAN intergration.

3. How to Promote Student Exchange Programs at Hanoi Law University in the Context of ASEAN Integration: Some Suggestions

The Association of South East Asian Nations (ASEAN) was estalished on August 8, 1967 and since its birth ASEAN has continously developed.[19] The

---

[18] For the academic calendar of Nagoya University see http://en.nagoyau.ac.jp/academics/campus_life/calendar/index.html (last accessed on November 25, 2017).

[19] Currently, ASEAN has 11 official state members and Vietnam became an official member of ASEAN on July 28, 1995. For more details, see: http://asean.org/asean/about-asean/ (last accessed on November 25, 2017).

– 34 –

Cebu Declaration on the Acceleration of the Establishment of an ASEAN Community by 2015 signed in Cebu, the Philippines on January 13, 2007 marked an impressive development of ASEAN. In practice, the ASEAN Economic Community (or AEC) – one of the three pilars of the ASEAN Community was officially launched on December 31, 2015 and it is expected that the other two pillars of the ASEAN Community - ASEAN Political -Security Community and ASEAN Socio-cultural Community will be launched by 2020.[20] AEC has set out many important goals - one of which is to create a single market and production base through free flow of goods, services, investment, skilled labour and free flow of capital,[21] and of course, legal services, investment and skilled lawyers are not exceptional. For legal education, what has been implied from free flow of 'services, investment, skilled labour' is that in the near future, law graduates of any law school of an ASEAN member state (for example, Thammasat Law School in Bangkok, Thailand) are allowed to practise law in other member states (for example, Vietnam or Singapore) and vice versa.

In such context, legal education in the ASEAN region must serve to enhance the human capacity of the legal sector for ASEAN integration. Generally speaking, for ASEAN integration, it is expected that ASEAN lawyers must understand the process of regional integration and have the necessary knowledge and skills to facilitate the process. For this purpose, among many key issues, law schools in the region including Hanoi Law University must pay attention to student and staff mobility.

To promote student exchange programs among law schools in the region, we are of the opinion that despite the efforts of individual law schools, an international network to facilitate the collaboration among law schools in the region should be developed. For the case of Hanoi Law University, it has become an active member of Asian Law Institute (ASLI) – a network of law schools in

---

[20] For more details, see http://asean.org/asean-economic-community/ (last accessed on November 25, 2017).

[21] For more details, see http://www.asean.org/wp-content/uploads/images/2015/November/aec-page/AEC-Blueprint-2025-FINAL.pdf (last accessed on November 22, 2017).

Asia and law schools in other regions which are interested in Asian law teaching and research since 2007.[22] In practice, Hanoi Law University takes part in a range of ASLI activities such as participation in ASLI annual conferences and other workshops and forums held by ASLI or nominating faculty members for ASLI research fellowship. ASLI, however, is not exclusive to law schools in the ASEAN region as it now has about 80 law schools in the world as its members.[23] ASLI, therefore, cannot focus on the issues of law schools in the ASEAN region and a similar network (Association of ASEAN Law Schools, for example) to facilitate the collaboration of ASEAN Law Schools should be soon established.[24]

First of all, such a network may help deal with several academic issues to promote student exchange programs, which noticeably are curriculum development and lecturer capacity building. As noted in the case of Hanoi Law University, the difficulties in developing and delivering courses taught in English caused several problems for implementing student exchange programs. Under the network, the member law schools will be able to collaborate with each other by sharing experiences and resources to overcome the above-mentioned problems.

With regard to the question of what courses taught in English should be included into the curriculum to support student exchange programs, it is suggested that the following courses should be offered by the law schools in the region including Hanoi Law University:

(i) Some courses which feature local laws and legal cultures: These courses offer exchange students some basic understandings of the law and legal culture of the host country in the region, enlarging their knowledge of the various legal systems in ASEAN. The course entitled "Introduction to the Vietnamese Legal

---

[22] For more details, see: https://law.nus.edu.sg/asli/members.html (last accessed on November 21, 2017).

[23] List of ASLI member is available at https://law.nus.edu.sg/asli/member_institutions.aspx (last accessed on November 25, 2017).

[24] Collaboration in legal education was also discussed by R.Rajeswaran in "*Legal Education in ASEAN in the 21ˢᵗ Century*", available at https://www.aseanlawassociation.org/9GAdocs/w2_Malaysia.pdf (last accessed on November 25, 2017).

– 36 –

System" which is currently offered by Hanoi Law University is an example. This course covers main topics related to the law and legal culture of Vietnam together with opportunities to visit different state agencies such as the Office of the National Assembly, the Supreme People's Court or the Ministry of Justice, to witness local courts hearing cases and to talk with legal practioners at local law firms for some understanding of the Vietnamese legal culture.

(ii) Some common international and regional issues related law courses such as International Trade Law, International Dispute Resolution, ASEAN Community Law, or ASEAN Investment Law: Ideally, these courses should be jointly developed by the law schools in the region under the network and then are included into their curriculum. By doing so, the experiences and resources to develop and deliver the courses can be effectively shared among the law schools in the region and the opportunities for exchange students will certainly be increased.

To effectively teach and study the above-mentioned courses in English, several technical supports for the law schools in the region are needed. For the courses of category (i) as mentioned above, an open English database of legal information of ASEAN countries should be further developed to assist students and teachers of the courses.[25] For the courses of category (ii), the ideas of using Massive Open Online Courses (MOOCs) and related techniques to develop and deliver the courses may be considered to attract more students of the law schools in the region. It is noted that for those technical supports, the law schools in the region may seek the assistance of other partners outside the network which already have had experiences and resources to do similar things. In this regard, some partner law schools of Japan like the Faculty of Law, Nagoya University and the Law School, Keio University which are interested in collaborating with ASEAN Law Schools should be good suggestions.

For lecturer capacity building, under the network of ASEAN Law Schools,

---

[25] In practice, some information of the Legal Systems in ASEAN is offered by ASEAN Law Association at http://www.aseanlawassociation.org/legal.html (last accessed on November 25, 2017). The data, especially those related to the legal systems of Vietnam, Cambodia, Myanmar, and Lao PDR, however, are still poor and further improvements are certainly needed.

teaching and research visits of law lecturers in the region should be encouraged by different incentives of both home and host law schools. Through such visits, law lecturers have good opportunities to enrich their knowledge of law and society of the host country, to share teaching and research experiences with their host colleagues and to improve their language skills which are very important for delivering courses in English.

Not only the academic matters, the network may also help overcome institutional differences and difficulties facing the law schools in the region and their students during the course of implementing student exchange programs. Within the network, law schools in the region may enter into bilateral or multilateral agreements to deal with the issues of hamonisation of degree structure, credit system, quality assurance and other institutional matters, which then help run smoothly student exchange programs. Collaboration of law schools under the network may also help seeking financial assistance from different sources to support exchange students and academic staff for teaching and research visits.

4. Conclusion

Hanoi Law University as a leading law school of Vietnam has made its big efforts to promote international collaboration towards the goal of university internationalisation. In the context of globalisation and international integration, what Hanoi Law University has done for this mission should be commendable given the fact that various challenges facing Vietnamese higher education institutions in general and Vietnamese law schools in particular still remain. The process of globalisation and international integration, however, presents not only challenges but also many opportunities. Within the region, opportunities for collaboration and promotion of legal education are open to Hanoi Law University and its partner law schools and the implementation of student exchange programs at Hanoi Law University should be promoted by taking advantage of these opportunities. Bearing this in mind, it is suggested that a network of the ASEAN law schools should be developed to assist Hanoi Law University and its partner law schools in overcoming all related problems, moving forward to the effective implementation of student exchange programs.

Appendix 1: List of current partners of Hanoi Law University

1	China University of Political Science and Law, China
2	Yunnan University, China
4	Zhongnan University of Law and Economics, Wuhan, China
5	National Taiwan University
6	National Judicial Academy, Lao PDR
7	The University of Melbourne, Australia
8	La Trobe University, Australia
9	The University of New South Wales, Australia
10	University of Göttingen, Germany
11	Justus Liebig University Giessen, Germany
12	Berlin University of Applied Sciences (HTW, Berlin), Germany
13	Free University of Berlin, Germany
14	Nagoya University, Japan
15	Keio University, Japan
16	University of Leeds, UK
17	National University of Singapore
18	Akron University, US
19	The All-Russian State University of Justice, Russia
20	Saint Petersburg University, Russia
21	The Peoples' Friendship University of Russia, Russia
22	The Russian Presidential Academy of National Economy and Public Administration under the President of the Russian Federation
23	Moscow State Institute of International Relations (MGIMO University), Russia
24	Kyungpook University, Korea
25	Yeungnam University, Korea
26	University of Waikato, New Zealand
27	The University of Szeged, Hungary
29	The Institute for Law and Finance , Goethe University Frankfurt am Main, Germany

Appendix 2: Outbound and inbound students under the one-semester student exchange program at Hanoi Law University
(2012-2017)

No	Home University	Host University	Year	Number of students
1	Hanoi Law University	National University of Singapore	2013	01
2	Hanoi Law University	National University of Singapore	2014	01
3	Hanoi Law University	La Trobe University, Australia	2014	01
4	Hanoi Law University	Nagoya University, University	2014	01
5	Nagoya University, Japan	Hanoi Law University	2014	01
6	Hanoi Law University	National University of Taiwan	2014	01
7	Hanoi Law University	National University of Taiwan	2015	02
8	Hanoi Law University	Nagoya University, Japan	2015	01
9	Hanoi Law University	National University of Taiwan	2016	03
10	Hanoi Law University	National University of Singapore	2016	01
11	Hanoi Law University	Nagoya University, Japan	2016	02
12	Nagoya University, Japan	Hanoi Law University	2016	01
13	Hanoi Law University	Keio University, Japan	2017	02
14	Hanoi Law University	Akron University, Ohio, US	2017	02
15	Hanoi Law University	Nagoya University, Japan	2017	01

Appendix 3: Outbound and inbound students under the short-term student exchange program at Hanoi Law University
(2012-2017)

No	Home University	Host University	Year	Number of students
1	Hanoi Law University	Nagoya University, Japan	2012	05
2	HTW, Berlin, Germany	Hanoi Law University	2012	10
3	MGIMO, Russia	Hanoi Law University	2013	01
4	Hanoi Law University	Nagoya University, Japan	2013	07
5	HTW, Berlin, Germany	Hanoi Law University	2013	10
6	Nagoya University, Japan	Hanoi Law University	2014	05
7	HTW, Berlin, Germany	Hanoi Law University	2014	10
8	Hanoi Law University	Nagoya University, Japan	2014	05
9	Nagoya University, Japan	Hanoi Law University	2015	05
10	HTW, Berlin, Germany	Hanoi Law University	2015	10
11	Hanoi Law University	Nagoya University	2015	06
12	HTW, Berlin, Germany	Hanoi Law University	2016	10
13	Hanoi Law University	Nagoya University	2016	07
14	Nagoya University, Japan	Hanoi Law University	2016	05
15	HTW, Berlin, Germany	Hanoi Law University	2017	10

Chapter 2

EXCHANGE PROGRAMS AS METHOD OF COMPARATIVE LEGAL STUDY:

UEL's Experience

Nguyen Ngoc Dien*

(University of Economics and Law Hochiminh city — Vietnam)

1. Interest of Comparative Law Study

Improvement of legal vision. Comparative law is developed as part of the legal curriculum in all law schools nowadays. In this subject, students are invited to discover the global picture of legal cultures as well as the particularities and originalities of some interesting legal concepts developed in other countries.

In the context of globalization, the acquisition of comparative legal knowledge attracts a lot of interest. First of all, it is helpful for students to acknowledge the panorama of legal systems and how to identify the characteristics of a national legal system from a global perspective . A student that has a solid understanding of comparative law is aware of the diversity of solutions for legal issues when analyzing his national law, and is able to improve his or her critical thinking skills and constructive spirit. A legal expert that possesses rich knowledge of foreign laws is able to better share information at international conferences and play an active role in international transactions and services.

Exchange program as means of comparative legal education. There are

---

* Professor and Vice-Rector of University of Economics and Law in HCM city.

two effective ways to study the national laws of another country: invite a legal expert from the subject country to teach at a local university or go to the subject country to study.

The first way is suitable for specialized group study in the framework of a master's program or higher level study. It is indeed more reasonable, especially in terms of cost, and efficient, for specialized study take place in the familiar classrooms of the home university with lectures given by a visiting professor, rather than to move the whole class abroad to follow the same lectures given by the same professor.

The second way is most suitable for interested students at the undergraduate and graduate levels. An undergraduate student would have the opportunity to learn many things by participating in foreign classes and consequently being exposed to different environments. In addition, student staying in the concerned country for a reasonable time would have the opportunity to discover the local culture by way of participating in social and community activities. Social and cultural knowledge that acquired in this practical way would be helpful for the comprehension of the solutions to legal issues developed by the host nation's lawmakers. A high level student with similar interests, could also acquire knowledge through courses at the host university.

2. Challenges and Solution

Challenges. Studying abroad is ordinarily something expensive and difficult. It is expensive because student must pay for travel and living costs during his/her stay in foreign country. It is also difficult because the student has to learn to live in an another country, where almost everything is not familiar to him or her and, thus, he or she has to adapt first for survival, and then to successfully complete the course of study.

Solution: Development of Exchange Programs. The development of exchange programs on the basis of institutional collaboration between related legal educational institutions is considered to be one of the best ways to ensure the effectiveness of comparative legal education.

Collaboration will enable better organization of the student's experience. Students enrolled in and selected to participate in the exchange program are grouped and placed under inter-institutional management during their study at the host university. More particularly, assistance may be provided by the host university to help foreign students adapt and integrate more rapidly to the host environment and spend a reasonable amount of time and effort on studying.

Mostly, an exchange program allows participating students to move to and live in host country in group. That better facilitates students' mutual assistance if the need arises.

3. Illustration: UEL—Paris 2 Exchange Programme

The UEL- Paris 2 Exchange Programme has been active since 2010. This program is composed of two wings—the exchange of students and the exchange of teachers.

3.1 Exchange of Teachers

The exchange of teachers is performed in accordance with the most popular model: teachers are invited by the partner university to stay for certain period of time in the host country to give lectures. Their courses are considered to be part of the regular training program of the host university. Most of the time, the teacher in charge of the concerned training program at the host university tries to determine the subject matter to be taught from a comparative point of view and then sends his request for a visiting professor to the partner university; the latter launches a call for candidates and proceeds with selection among the candidates.

Normally, the host university pays the airfare and accommodation of the visiting professor.

– 43 –

3.2 Exchange of Students

The exchange of students is much more remarkable, especially on account of the diversity of student's objectives, the particularities of the training program and teaching methods, the gradual increase in the number of participants, and the social impact of the program.

Student's objectives. On the French side, all students participating in the exchange program are motivated by the desire to acquire knowledge of the Vietnamese legal system and culture. However, the individual's final objective may not be the same: one student may just be curious to learn; another participant plans to prepare himself seriously with the scientific knowledge and living experience for his or her future professional life.

On the Vietnamese side, most students participating in the exchange program are interested in obtaining a foreign academic degree. Such an academic title is expected to be useful for their future careers.

Development and performance of the training program. Consequently, the methods of selection for the students participating in the exchange program, the determination of the length of study, and the conception of the training program are not the same from the French and Vietnamese perspectives.

On the French side, the students participating in the exchange program are junior (third-year) or senior (fourth-year) students. The total number of French students participating in the program is around thirty per year. The majority of these students are seniors. In accordance with the agreement between the two universities, junior students stay at the host university for the whole academic year, and senior students only for the first semester of the academic year.

On the Vietnamese side, students participating in the exchange program are seniors or recipients of a bachelor's degree. They all stay at the host university for the whole academic year.

As for the training program, the Vietnamese students are enrolled in the relevant degree training program at the host university. They follow courses together with other students enrolled in the same program, and have to take the subject examination in accordance with the general regulations. In general, they are totally integrated in the students' community of the host university.

As for French students, the host university organizes special classes, where they work together with the Vietnamese students who are interested in the same courses.

For each subject, the training is divided into two parts – lectures given by a professor and a presentation of research paper by the students. Concerning lectures, the professor is requested to introduce interesting Vietnamese legal concepts and compare them with the corresponding French legal concepts. Therefore, it is necessary for the teacher have good knowledge of both Vietnamese and French law. Where there are remarkable similarities or differences between the two legal systems, the teacher must provide the necessary explanations, according to dominant doctrine, as well as personal opinion to clarify the comparison.

Concerning the research paper, the students are invited to determine a subject that fits his or her study interests, provided that it is relevant to the courses he chose in the framework of the training program. The questions raised in the course of research must be treated from comparative point of view. After a presentation is completed in the classroom, classmates are invited to provide comments or/and raise questions and the speaker has to provide an immediate response. The teacher appreciates the quality of the research paper as well as its presentation, and then provides a score that normally accounts for 40% of the final grade in the concerned subject matter; the remaining 60% is awarded in a final examination. The students' records are transferred to the students' university of origin for validation.

In addition to class attendance, students are involved in cultural and sportif activities, so that they can have the opportunity experience daily local life.

Impact of the Program. The exchange program developed collaboratively by UEL and Paris 2 over more than ten years has attracted more and more participants. From the Vietnamese perspective, it is one of the most successful exchange programs. It contributes to the promotion of a Vietnamese university's image on international level thanks to the positive foreign students' feedback. Vietnamese students, having participated in this program, received a degree from Paris and then returned to Vietnam to be engaged in teaching or legal professional activities. This contributes to the improvement of the quality of legal education and legal practice in Vietnam.

4. Experience

The success of the UEL-Paris 2 Exchange Programme is the result of both partners' efforts. The key reasons for success are as follows:

- Taking serious consideration of students' needs in the field of comparative legal study and preparing the program to provide an opportunity for students to satisfy individual study objectives;
- Stimulating students' curiosity to discover the differences between the law of related jurisdictions;
- Organizing students' stay with special care and encouraging students to be integrated in the host university and life in the host country overall.

Chapter 3

INTERNATIONAL EXCHANGE PROGRAM(S) FOR LEGAL EDUCATION AT THE FACULTY OF LAW AND PUBLIC AFFAIRS OF PAÑÑĀSĀSTRA UNIVERSITY OF CAMBODIA

Kong Phallack*
Phin Sovath**

(Paññāsāstra University)

1. Introduction to Paññāsāstra University of Cambodia and the Faculty of Law and Public Affairs

Paññāsāstra University of Cambodia (PUC) is a private university established on September 9, 1997. A law program was started in 2002 and is now known as the Faculty of Law and Public Affairs (FLPA) or the Paññāsāstra Law School (SALA CHBAB PANNHASASTRA in Khmer). It is a relatively new law school and has been in operation for almost 15 years. All courses are conducted in English, but the FLPA has provided some backup courses in both Khmer and

---

* KONG Phallack is the Dean and a professor of law at the Faculty of Law and Public Affairs, Paññāsāstra University of Cambodia (PUC); managing partner and attorney at law at KhmerLex Legal Solutions, a locally established law firm; and arbitrator of the Arbitration Council. He has handled 780 cases among the 2,684 cases registered at the Arbitration Council. Dr. KONG Phallack used to serve as Chairman of the Board of Directors of the Arbitration Council for two mandates.

** PHIN Sovath is an Assistant Dean and professor of law at the Faculty of Law and Public Affairs, Paññāsāstra University of Cambodia (PUC); partner and attorney at law of Bun & Associates, a locally established law firm; and arbitrator and Vice President of the National Commercial Arbitration Center (NCAC).

– 47 –

English[1] for the students so that they are able to work in Cambodia, especially if they want to sit for the bar exam or for other exams of other schools that use Khmer as the main language, for example, the Royal Academy for Judicial Professions (RAJP)[2] and the Royal School of Administration (ERA). Royal School of Administration [RSA] or Ecole Royale Administration [ERA] and exams offered by the governmental ministries or institution to become civil servants.

The FLPA strives to deliver quality legal education that is accessible to and responsive to the needs of the people of Cambodia as well as the global community. We place special emphasis on research and studies in law, social justice, and policy. As a law school, our mission is to produce a wide variety of human resources for the 21st century through a curriculum grounded in the principles of multidisciplinarism, internationalism, and pioneerism.

The FLPA has an established and internationally recognized reputation for excellence in teaching law in English. The FLPA's faculty members care about their teaching and see students as a priority. It provides a unique opportunity for high quality legal education. Rather than just telling people how we are doing things differently and better, the FLPA is committed to making it obvious that it is student-centered and devoted to preparing students to enter professional schools and the job market as well as for further study overseas.

Currently, the FLPA provides legal education to students through three programs: the Bachelor Program (LL.B.), the Master Program (LL.M.), and the Doctoral Program (LL.D./Ph.D.). In the LL.M. Program, students can choose among three majors: LL.M. in International Human Rights Law, LL.M. in International Business Law, and LL.M. in Intellectual Property Law. For the Doctoral Program, we offer both a professional program, at the end of which students will receive a Doctor of Laws degree (LL.D.), and a research program, at the end of

---

[1] Courses: Legal terminologies are taught under the course titled "Basic Concepts of Law & Fundamental Codes" [Civil Code, Code of Civil Procedures, Criminal Code, and Code of Criminal Procedures].

[2] The RAJP is composed of the School of Judges and Prosecutors, the School of Court Clerks, the School of Notaries, and the School of Bailiffs.

which students will receive a Doctor of Philosophy (Ph.D.) in law.[3]

In addition to these programs, FLPA has also set up a legal clinic to help students develop and enhance their practical skills. This year, FLPA has just launched a new legal clinic program called the "Rights of Persons with Disabilities," which is open to both bachelor's and master's students who are interested in the rights of people with disabilities.

2. Why an International Exchange Program?

This is a very interesting question, one that has been under continuous discussion for many years. Before we can provide any answers, we first need to define what an international exchange program entails? Does the word "international" indicate that it is between nations, between universities, or between institutions? Does the term "exchange" mean an exchange between and among professors, students, knowledge, and skills? What kind of program should be established to benefit the partner universities?

There is also the related question of why a university would be interested in cooperating with another university, in particular if one university is weak and the other university is strong. Generally, if a university is very weak, other universities are unlikely to want to cooperate with it; arguably, a strong university may instead just want to use the weak university for their own benefit. In such a case, an international exchange program is just on paper, and there will be no real implementation.

Whenever a strong university approaches the FLPA for an international exchange program, we usually provide a frank statement that we are a new university and are very weak. In addition, the FLPA always desires a real implementation program before entering into a memorandum of understanding (MoU) with

---

[3] For details of each of the programs, please visit the website of the FLPA, available at http://law.puc.edu.kh/index.php/law-programs (last visited on Nov. 30, 2017).

any partner university. FLPA does not want to have the MoU just be a marketing tool without any practical outcome. We are approached by many international institutes to discuss cooperation. However, the FLPA needs a real implementation program. We need collaboration, not cooperation. The FLPA believes that collaboration between two schools or institutions can be fruitful for and beneficial to both schools or institutions. Therefore, even if the FLPA is weak and our partner university is strong, we try our best to support the partner university.

Finally, we believe that the abbreviation for an International Exchange Program, "IEP," can also mean "I Empower the Partners." Even though we are weak, we still empower our strong partner university. If our partner university is strong, they should try to empower us in return. If each partner grows, we should be proud of each other. All of the above forms the basis on which the FLPA considers whether to enter into an MoU with any partner university.

3. Outputs and Outcomes

Since its establishment, the PUC has entered into many international exchange programs with many partner universities around the world. The PUC serves as an academic bridge between universities in Cambodia and those overseas. We have established formal and informal linkages, networking, and technical cooperation with numerous universities and institutions in the U.S., Europe, and the Asia-Pacific region. Below is a list of those programs:[4]

- The U.S. (32 universities and institutions)
- Europe (9 universities and institutions)
- Asia and ASEAN[5] (80 universities and institutions)
- New Zealand (1 university)

---

[4] For a specific cooperation program, please see the PUC website available at http://www.puc.edu.kh/index.php/international (last visited on Nov. 30, 2017).

[5] Association of Southeast Asia Nations: ASEAN

– 50 –

INTERNATIONAL EXCHANGE PROGRAM(S) FOR LEGAL EDUCATION
AT THE FACULTY OF LAW AND PUBLIC AFFAIRS OF PAÑÑĀSĀSTRA UNIVERSITY OF CAMBODIA

- The U.K. (5 universities)
- Australia (3 universities)
- Russia (1 university)

All of these cooperation programs, most of which involve international cooperation, take different forms. Here is a list of the forms of cooperation we have used
so far with partner universities:

- **MoU**: Memorandum of Understanding
- **MOA**: Memorandum of Agreement
- **AOC**: Agreement of Cooperation
- **EPA**: Educational Partnership Agreement
- **IA**: Institutional Agreement
- **MMCP**: Minutes of Meeting Collaboration Program
- **JVA**: Joint Venture Agreement
- **ICA**: Intercollegiate Cooperation Agreement
- **GCA**: General Cooperation Agreement
- **GA**: General Agreement
- **MOC**: Memorandum of Cooperation
- **CA**: Cooperation Agreement
- **EA**: Exchange Agreement
- **AD**: Addendum

Even though we use various forms of international cooperation, the question
is how such cooperation has been implemented and what results have been obtained from such implementation. In addition to these forms, there is also a form
of case-by-case cooperation. In this last form, there is no written MoU at all;
however, in a sense the agreement is stronger because it is entered into with real
commitment and understanding. It is about the human connection, trust, honesty,
and commitment, which are key to a fruitful international exchange program.

At the FLPA level, we have also had cooperation with other law schools,
universities, and institutions in the form of MoUs or MOAs. For example, with
the Raoul Wallenberg Institute of Human Rights and Humanitarian Law (RWI),

based in Lund, Sweden, we have the ability to exchange professors, students, library, research, and a legal clinic program. Another example is our cooperation with the Southeast Asian Human Rights Studies Network (SEAHRN), where we focus more on human rights, education, and international law. Below is the list of the FLPA's cooperation with partners that has resulted in fruitful outcomes, with an indication of what was exchanged:

- The Raoul Wallenberg Institute of Human Rights and Humanitarian Law (RWI): professors, students, library, research, legal clinic program
- The Southeast Asian Human Rights Studies Network (SEAHRN): education, conference, networking of professors
- The Human Rights Resource Center (HRRC): research, publications
- The Open Society Justice Initiative (OSJI): legal clinic program
- The Konrad-Adenauer-Stiftung (KAS): annual law talk, publications
- SHEAPSEA: teaching collaboration, research
- BABSEA: clinical legal education
- Handong International University (HIU): graduate student
- Bridgewater State University: student exchange
- Keio Law School (KLS): exchange program

These cooperation programs has provided mutual benefits to both FLPA and its partners , in particular the students and professors, They are examples of the successfully implementation programs. The FLPA is not looking for a large number of cooperation programs, but we do want to have real partners and effective implementation. The table below is a summary of the achievements of such programs between 2016 and 2017.

1. Students

LL.B. (3)	LL.M. (7)
- 1 (BSU, USA) - 2 (KLS, Japan)	- 5 (Lund, Sweden) - 2 (KLS, Japan)

2. Professors and Staff

Professors (1)	Staff (3)
- 1 (Lund, Sweden)	- 2 (Lund, Sweden) - 1 (KLS, Japan)

INTERNATIONAL EXCHANGE PROGRAM(S) FOR LEGAL EDUCATION
AT THE FACULTY OF LAW AND PUBLIC AFFAIRS OF PAÑÑĀSĀSTRA UNIVERSITY OF CAMBODIA

3. Teaching Collaboration PUC-FLPA & VNU, Hanoi, School of Law

Students	LL.M. in PUC-FLPA and VNU, Hanoi
Professors	3 International Professors (Vietnam, Thailand, The Philippines) 1 Professor from Ohio Law School, USA teaching International Labor Law to L.L.M Students.

4. Good Practice

In these cooperation programs, we believe that we have achieved good practice with many partner universities and institutions, including the RWI, SEAHRN, KLS, OSJI, KAS, HRRC, SHAPESEA, and BABSEA and case by case with committed individuals from respective institutions. For example, we are proud of our cooperation with the KLS. We even started without an MoU, but we wanted to see this cooperation happen. We started to discuss an MoU, but at the same time, our activities and their results made the commitment of each partner evident.

This kind of practice has arisen from the past experience of international trade between Cambodia and China and India. There were no written documents or authorities, but trade was nevertheless conducted. In this sense, what we call good practice is a cooperation from the heart, and they are conducted in good faith and mutual respect. The result is both partners being happy.

Another example is our cooperation with BABSEA on clinical legal education. BABSEA is the founder and leading provider of clinical legal education in Cambodia and the region. They started the clinic in Cambodia, where we tried to set up the first clinical legal education in Asia. The main reason for establishing this kind of education is to make a difference.

5. Challenges of International Exchange Programs

We divide these challenges into different categories. The first category of challenges arises from the management of the law school. We see this challenge when we support students or when we implement exchange programs. The first issue is visa and travel arrangements. For a country like Japan, where it takes only a week to receive the visa and information on the website is clear, this can be fine. However, for other countries that are very strict, it is difficult for our students.

We sometimes use another network to obtain visa for our students. One of our students intended to study in Lund. The application process at the university was very slow. The student needed the visa at least two or three weeks before the start of the university term, but the visa had not yet been released. In fact, it was not the Swedish Embassy that issued the visa for Lund but another embassy. In the European system, they send the jobs to a different embassy to hand out the visas for different countries. Therefore, we have to find other ways to assist our students to get their visas, otherwise, the visas may not arrive on time.

Another major challenge is the school admission and requirements. Such requirements may be much higher in developed countries than in our country. As a result, it is a bit difficult for Cambodian students to get admitted to foreign universities like Keio University. We are also not sure whether students at foreign universities are interested in coming to study with us. If they come to study with us, what are the benefits for them? In our experience, we have so far received only two Filipino students [1 in LL.B. and 1 in LL.M.] one Japanese student, enrolled in the business law course, because his parents were working in Cambodia. In addition, a Malaysian student registered for the business law course because her father runs a business in Cambodia. In sum, foreign students come when they have relatives or friends working or doing business in Cambodia.

The residential and living environment is another key challenge. In general, when you enter a foreign country, you may find it a bit difficult to rent a house and to get to know all the local systems. For example, if a student goes to live in

INTERNATIONAL EXCHANGE PROGRAM(S) FOR LEGAL EDUCATION
AT THE FACULTY OF LAW AND PUBLIC AFFAIRS OF PAÑÑĀSĀSTRA UNIVERSITY OF CAMBODIA

Japan, they should learn and understand the concept of "key money": what it is and why they need to pay money for the key. In Cambodia, we do not have this concept; we just have a deposit that is returned on departure.

The learning environment in Japan is very technologically equipped compared with Cambodia. The curriculum, grading system, language, and cultural shock are related challenges, but some of these problems can be easily resolved. For example, we sent our students to study in Lund for a semester exchange; since even the grading system is different, we addressed the issue of, for example, how an A grade in Lund would be transferred to an A grade at the PUC in the MoU. Although we have different grading systems, we can use an agreement to easily solve the problem.

Financial support is a big issue for people from Cambodia if they want to go to a foreign university, even a nearby university in Laos, Vietnam, or Taiwan. However, when we had a conference in Ho Chi Minh City, our students were able to cover the cost because we could travel by car or bus and find cheaper accommodation. Therefore, for a kind of international exchange between neighboring countries for a short course of one week, the financial issue can be easily solved. Commitment from the partner university and support from the top management are also big issues because each university has a different system to run and manage the program.

Another category of challenges arises from our students who went to study in the United States, Japan, Korea, and Lund. Their challenges are not much different from the challenges of the management of the law school which were raised in this report. One interesting challenge is the problem of transport. They do not know how to ride the subway or a bus. To solve this, they are given information by the organizer to help them exit the airport and navigate onwards transport. In Lund, everyone used their credit cards; they hardly used cash.

Similarly, there are issues concerning the selection of students and the documentation process for students who want to study abroad. When they come home, students also need to follow up as to whether their grades have been released and transferred. For international students who study abroad normally, we get support from the university which releases the temporary grade and may be officially recognized by the other universities.

6. Conclusions

As discussed above, to make any international exchange program work effectively and successfully, it is very important to have real cooperation or collaboration with concrete action plans. It is very important that we do not only enter into an agreement on paper, but we expect concrete outcomes arising from the implementation of such agreement.

We have discussed a number of challenges, some of which result from the context of one particular country or from countries experiencing different individual challenges and some of which result from partner universities being at different stages (for example, one university still being at the early stage without much experience with exchange programs, while the other already has extensive experience of partnering with other universities in developed countries). For such reasons, the expectations from partner universities may be different. Accordingly, it is important that when we start to implement—or even before implementing—any collaboration or cooperation programs, we look into the curriculum.

We have to reform that curriculum to fit what we expect in that program. For example, the credit transfer and grading system is very important, not only for the partner university but also for students, in particular to motivate more students to apply to these exchange programs.

All the challenges can be addressed, but the question is how to address them. In our view, it is important to improve or develop additional resources, in particular guidelines, tools, or instructions. One common pitfall is a single set of guidelines being applied to all exchange programs. Instead, guidelines should be specific to one program, one country, and one university because sometimes when a general set of instructions or guidelines is applied to a partner university, it does not work well. Therefore, it is also important that we revisit or improve our tools, programs, or instructions to make sure that they respond to the needs of the students and the partner universities.

Finally, our students are interested not only in learning about the local systems and law but also about how to practice law. The ultimate outcome for students after graduation is to go into work; in other words, they have to practice law in this country. Therefore, to have students develop all of practical skills, in particular through an international exchange program, it is important that we also extend our focus further to internships and externships in law firms or companies. In particular, in Cambodia, where legislation and case law are not widely available to the public, it is hard for students to learn the law in practice. Therefore, even though we exchange through the university at an academic level, without all of this there probably are limitations.

We are not sure if this is also applicable to Laos or Myanmar as we are at an early stage of legal information disclosure. Because of this, we believe that it is very important that we promote externship or internship programs in the exchange program. Students should also have three- or six-month internships in a law firm so that they can learn from real legal practitioners.

To implement it, we should start thinking about how we can promote these externship or internship programs. In particular, we are concerned about information dissemination, for example, how a student at Keio Law School can find out that there is the opportunity for an internship in Cambodia, Laos, or Thailand. Therefore, we probably have to think about how to develop a tool or database to share all of these opportunities with students at the university as a partner university. This is just a simple example of what we can start from now in the current international exchange program. Partner universities should collaborate further to study and develop these externship or internship programs comprehensively and practically for students by taking into account the context of each country and the different levels of commitment and capacity of each partner university.

Chapter 4

THE CHALLENGES TO STUDY LAW ABROAD:
The International Cooperation and Exchange Program
for Legal Education at The Faculty of Law and Political science,
National University of Laos

Viengvilay Thiengchanhxay*
Sonenaly Nanthavong**
(National University of Laos)

1. Introduction

National University of Laos (NUOL) is a leading university in Lao PDR. It is located in Dongdok Campus (main campus university) and consists of 13 faculties[1], 2 institutes, 1 central library, 3 centers, 1 hospital, 11 offices, and 1 School for Gifted and Ethnic Students which comes under the Ministry of Education and Sports (MoES). At present, the NUOL works closely with other universities to promote quality national and international cooperation of the country. In addition, human resource development is also a key to achieving our goals, vision and mission of NUOL's educational development plan from 2016 -2020[2].

---

* Associate Professor, Dean of the Faculty of Law and Political Science, National University of Laos.

** Head of International Cooperation Unit, Faculty of Law and Political Science, National University of Laos.

[1] 13 Faculties of National University of Laos : Faculty of Agriculture; Faculty of Architecture; Faculty of Economics and Business Management; Faculty of Education; Faculty of Engineering; Faculty of Environmental Sciences; Faculty of Forestry; Faculty of Law and Political Sciences; Faculty of Language Education; Faculty of Natural Sciences; Faculty of Social Sciences; Faculty of Water Resources; and Faculty of Sport Sciences.

[2] 6 Strategic Plans 2016 -2020: (1) develop NUOL human resource with high professional and

– 59 –

The NUOL is strongly committed to providing quality training in higher education. The goals set are to ensure that students become well-trained and disciplined academics, highly skilled and knowledgeable professionals, and trained graduates who are expected to become specialists and experts in their fields of training whereby they can commit and contribute back to their country's socio-economic endeavor. It is with this link to the regional and international norms and standards of development that the university developed its comprehensive management system with full efficiency and transparency. NUOL also aims to become a full-fledged university and green campus with the developed infrastructure, facilities and resources fully provided for the academic training needs. By NUOL goals, every faculty will be required to compete for foreign aid and to collaborate with counterparts from the world.

The Faculty of Law and Political Science (FLP) is one of the faculty members of the National University of Laos that promotes the legal teaching and promotion of the Rule of Law in Lao PDR. Therefore, FLP needs to have the co-operation with universities, organizations and other institutes both internal and external in order to promote academic framework to regional and international standards. Moreover, FLP students are also encouraged to apply for scholarships with our counterparts and others who support and provide information. However, Lao legal exchange students are faced with some challenges because of different education system, the process of credit transfer, the learning conditions and other international programs as well.

---

academic knowledge competence; (2) manage the resources suitable to the socio-economic development; (3) upgrade and improve the teaching and learning quality catching up with regional and international standards; (4) conduct researches and academic services to fulfill the requirement of socio-economic development; (5) upgrade and expand the infrastructure facilitating educational development; (6) Promote quality national and international cooperation.

2. International Cooperation and Exchange Program at FLP, NUOL

2.1 International Cooperation

The National University of Laos's cooperation with its partners is achieved through general agreement on cooperation and partnerships signed with universities, institutes, agencies and organizations in the region and the world. In 2017, MOU - based cooperation stands at about 250 with Asia, ASEAN and Europe countries, with the following cooperation:

1. Developing its human resources both in the academic and administrative fields;

2. Promoting joint research and organizing seminars and symposiums;

3. And exchanging scientific data and related publications in all disciplinary fields.

The International Relations and cooperation is regarded as the NUOL's key roles in its functions and it is to ensure the effective coordination and cooperation with the external partners and networks in different levels. NUOL is strengthening its effort in international affairs and this is in line with the Government's policy on international relations which is based on mutual benefits and non-interference in mutual internal affairs. To ensure efficient implementation of internal and external relations and cooperation tasks, the NUOL has adopted the following Strategic Development Plans:

- Review regulations and practices on internal and external relations and cooperation of the NUOL, roles and responsibilities with the tasks and activities related;

- Review and improve system for appropriate and relevant practices in accordance with the roles and responsibilities; and

- Review and improve the coordinating system with the unit or division in charge as to ensure the regular and effective coordination with the parties and authorities concerned.

- Review the existing regulations and make new regulations and principles which are more relevant and practical for the NUOL's international relations and cooperation tasks' implementation in connection to the Party Central Committee's policy and guidelines as well as the university's requirements. (2016-2020)

In the academic years 2015 – 2017, there was a large number of students' exchange within ASEAN/AUN, ASEAN plus 3 - Japan, Korea, and China. For example, the number of NUOL students exchange program within ASEAN/AUN indicated that 33 students in Singapore, 30 students in Thailand, 17 students in Malaysia, 4 students in the Philippines, 2 students in Indonesia, 2 students in Brunei Darussalam and 1 student in Vietnam. Another student exchange within ASEAN plus three – Japan, Korea and China are 27 students in Japan, 17 students in South Korea, and 18 students in China. The duration of these students exchange programs ranges from one week to one year. The courses are conducted in English as approved by the partner university, and the tuition fee is supported by the host university based on previously signed academic agreements. Host countries generally provide both partial and full scholarships. Furthermore, activities such as study trips student and cultural exchanges are also included. Exchange programs are open to students, lecturers and researchers, and it also includes other activities that have been agreed upon during the signing of the MoUs.

The Faculty of Law and Political Science or FLP has much cooperation with other universities, both locally and globally. It plays the significant role for our academic exchanges. At the present time, there are MOU and MOA signed with other law schools such as: Faculty of Law of Rajabhat Mahasarakham; Chiang Mai; North-Chiang Mai; Khon Kaen; Mae Fah Luang; Thammasat; and College of Politics and Governance, Mahasarakham University (Thailand); Faculty of Law, National University of Hanoi (Vietnam); Nagoya University and Law School of Keio University (Japan); School of Law of Jean Moulin Lyon 3 (France) and the Strengthening the Rule of Law of Luxembourg Development Project

(Lao/031) University of Luxembourg. This cooperation is based on one of the NUOL strategic development plan as internal and international relations and co-operation.

The core areas of cooperation consists of 5 main points :(1) Exchange staff/ faculty and students; (2) Exchange academic materials and publication; (3) Joint scientific research and academic activities; (4) Scholarships and human resources development and; (5) Participation in seminars and trainings.

Based on our signing MOU cooperation with partnerships and areas of mutual cooperation agreed, the Faculty of Law and Political Science is strengthening on implementing of exchange law lectures/students by joint the seminars, trainings, research projects and study visits with other counterparts both internal and external regions.

2.2 Legal Exchange Program

The legal exchange program is seen as a significant step in human resources development in Lao PDR. The scholarship study and training abroad are highly sought-after, especially for law students. The students from international relations department are very highly passionate and are always on the look-out for new experiences. Opportunities for student exchange came from various MoUs cooperation between universities/faculties, Embassies, European Union Support to Higher Education in the ASEAN Region (EU - SHARE) and other information from websites.

In the academic year 2016 – 2017, lecturers and students under FLP went for exchange programs based on the signed MoUs. FLP lecturers attended the seminars and exchanged teaching best practices with Khonkaen University. Two master students joined the seminars in Keio University, and two graduate students are now doing six - month exchange program in Nagoya University. Besides that, there are FLP students who have participated in Japanese language class. They also had the opportunity to exchange social and cultural learning in Nagoya University over a two – week period. Moreover, FLP lectures are continuously working with Japan International Cooperation Agency Project (JICA) on writing textbooks about criminal, civil, and civil law code. Other FLP student exchange programs involved students participating in both short and long term programs such as International Humanitarian Law Moot Court Competition in Hong Kong, the 3rd ASEAN Foundation Model ASEAN Meeting in the Philippines, Debate of Human Rights in Thailand, and Japan East Asia Network of Exchange for Students and Youths (JENESYS).

2.3 The Processes of Applying for and Selection on Exchange Programs

Lao students exchange program including Law students must be the students who are studying at National University of Laos. The students should be in the 2nd to 4th year and have achieved GPA 3.00 /4.00 (2.5 is also eligible in some programs). The selected students need to prepare necessary documents as follows:

1. Copy of valid passport.
2. Certificate of Enrolment / Attestation.
3. Official Transcripts.
4. Study Plan.
5. Letter of Recommendation.
6. Letter of Endorsement from home university.
7. Certificates of English Proficiency.
8. Certificates of Achievement (Optional)

Students can contact their own international relations office in each faculty and the main office at NUOL. Otherwise, they can ask the faculty news board or person in charge of academic affairs/student affairs. NUOL students can also apply from the NUOL's website as www.nuol.edu.la, which consists of three steps:

- Written and Interview
  - Written Assessment
  - Selection Interview
- Application Preparation
  - Complete Application

- Attach Supporting Documents
- Official Nomination
  - Official nomination
  - Submit original copy of application

Moreover, FLP students who apply for scholarships or have been selected by the faculty partnerships (MoUs), in principle, they will follow the rules of the National University of Laos and host universities.

Actually, there are many exchange programs at NUOL in the present time. For a semester/ one academic year, students can apply in Cambodia, Indonesia, Malaysia, Myanmar, The Philippines, Singapore, Thailand, Vietnam, Japan, Portugal, Europe and Korea. One week – Two months are in Singapore, Korea, Japan and Thailand.

In fact, under the SHARE Project, the applicant can apply to the following universities:

Royal University of Phnom Penh, Cambodia, University of Indonesia, Indonesia, University Kebangsaan, Malaysia, University of Yangon, Myanmar, University of Philippines, the Philippines, Chulalongkorn University, Thailand, and Vietnam National University, Hanoi, Vietnam.

Also, the students also apply for European universities as University of Ghent, Belgium, Tomas Bata Univeristy, Czech Republic, SGH Warsaw School of Economics, Poland and University College Cork, Ireland.

3. Outputs, Outcomes and Challenges

Although the FLP is a young institution, it has already developed intense activity in the field of international cooperation. FLP has developed working relations with a number of institutions worldwide. It has signed more than 10 different MoUs with universities from ASEAN member countries, as well as Japan, France and Luxembourg. Furthermore, as the member of the ASEAN University Network (AUN), the FLP of National University of Laos has actively engaged in a number of activities aiming at both academic and research development and cooperation among the AUN member universities as well as countries in the ASEAN region. This movement and contribution by the NUOL or FLP is regarded as an important input and part for Laos in preparation for the ASEAN Community by 2016.

By engaging with many partnerships, the FLP has achieved various outputs, outcomes and challenges as follow:

3.1 Outputs

At present, the FLP has been sent a large number of staff/lecturers and students on exchange and to join conferences. The outputs of these activities are to promote and raise the FLP's regional and international profile, and to disseminate Lao law and culture. Moreover, it is also to promote the capability of Law lecturers and students. Most law students are more encouraged and motivated in their work after their participation in the preliminary selection interview. Furthermore, the academic atmosphere and learning competitive awareness among students themselves within the NUOL are built up and that provides NUOL students with the opportunity to be exposed to best practices and also deepen their academic skills and adapting skills in new learning environments.

3.2 Outcomes

After participation in the conferences/exchange abroad, Lao law lecturers and students have gained better understanding of international law and teaching – learning systems of other countries. In addition, it enables them to gain a better understanding of the host country's politics, economics, society and culture. The exchange program is a significant part of students' university lives as it opens students vision, motivates them to put more effort to study in order to make their own country be more developed.

Moreover, when the Law students study short term and/or semester long program abroad, these studies found that students can improve their speaking proficiency during one semester. There is a positive relationship between students' integrative motivation and interaction with second language culture, and student contact with the host country's languages has a great effect on their speaking improvement.

3.3 Challenges

To study law abroad is a challenge for all Lao students but it is necessary for cooperation and development in legal study. The number of Lao exchange students has increased in recent years. Many of them found opportunities to upgrade themselves by participating in short - term studies, seminars and by embarking upon their Masters or Doctorate of Philosophy studies abroad. In addition, these scholars are being supported by their host countries and universities for which they have applied for their studies. The main issues and challenges for international cooperation to be addressed by Faculty of Law and Political Science, National University of Laos are:

- Less international programs offered in English and such practices in student exchanges with foreign partner universities.

- Students have low understanding of the English language.

- No appropriate credit transfer system to accept the student's grade and credit gained from exchange program.

- No undergraduate programs that are taught in English language.

- The exchange program management in cross-faculty is not well managed.

- Lack of financial support toward participation in seminars, training and student activities organizing overseas or at the partner universities. In other words, student exchange program at NUOL or FLP is scholarship-based from the host university; we are unable to participate in the program invited with self-support.

- Inadequate human resources, lack of staff to do the work;

- Lack of capacity possessed by staff, yet internal process or procedures concerning international cooperation and coordination remains as issues of improvement;

Sometimes, even though we have signed MoUs with many universities worldwide, we still lack real implementation because contact is not continuously maintained and there are difficulties on the budget, human resources and some facilities of our faculty. However, the FLP needs to build and develop the capacity of faculty members in order to promote them and build the international course for our academic exchange with partnerships.

4. Conclusion

The Faculty of Law and Political Science, National University of Laos is an important institution for legal studies which is under the Ministry of Education and Sports. Many undergraduate students would like to study in this faculty; so far in the light of quality assurance, a lot of candidates cannot pass easily. Nonetheless, the faculty has continued to compete for the grant support from other international universities and organizations in order to promote our faculty and students to upgrade their education. Moreover, FLP will continue to work hard by creating further cooperative joint programs with partner universities as well as to improve the regulations of the cooperation in the future.

Chapter 5

INTERNATIONAL EXCHANGE PROGRAMS AND COLLABORATIONS FOR LEGAL EDUCATION AT THAMMASAT UNIVERSITY

Junavit Chalidabhongse*
Viravat Chantachote**

(Thammasat University)

1. Introduction

Legal education is vitally important to social and economic development. In the globalized world, the business transactions with international elements have become increasingly essential and the lawyers capable of dealing with such transactions are highly demanded. The universities offering legal education have faced tremendous challenges to equip their students with legal knowledge and experience on both domestic and foreign laws. The activities that tend to facilitate such challenges are exchange programs and collaborations between universities so that knowledge can be shared and relations can be established, resulting in benefits to both students and universities.

This paper explains student exchange programs and various types of educational collaborations at Thammasat University Faculty of Law. It is organized into two main parts, namely, the part relating to the program taught in Thai

---

* Assistant Dean, Deputy Director of International Programs, Faculty of Law, Thammasat University, Thailand.

** Assistant Professor, Chairman of the Curriculum Development and Quality Assurance in Education, Faculty of Law, Thammasat University, Thailand.

language and the part relating to the programs taught in English language. The paper begins with an overview of the Thai-taught program in Section 2. Then, the barriers in current Thai-taught program with regard to exchange programs and collaborations will be explained in Section 3. Section 4 will show the main concepts of the new development of the Thai-taught program that would increase the likelihood of students to join exchange programs. We will then move to the part of law programs taught in English language. The overview of English-taught programs will be given in Section 5. Then, different models of exchange programs and collaborations in English-taught programs will be described in Section 6. Finally, the paper will be concluded in Section 7.

2. Overview of Law Programs Taught in Thai Language at Thammasat University Faculty of Law

The Faculty of Law at Thammasat University offers law degrees taught in Thai language in many levels, namely, Bachelor of Laws (LL.B.), Master of Laws (LL.M.) and Doctor of Laws (LL.D.).[1] In this paper, we will focus only on the Bachelor of Laws (LL.B.) as the students from such a program are majority of our students.

Let us begin with the explanation of the semester system being used at present. The Faculty of Law implements the semester system consisting of two regular semesters and one summer semester. The first semester runs from the middle of August to the end of December while the second semester begins in the middle of January and ends in the early of June. The summer semester, which is not mandatory, covers the period from the middle of June to the end of July.

The Thai-taught LL.B. program is a four-year program that requires at least 141 credits for graduation. One credit equals one hour of teaching per week. A course usually contains three credits and therefore requires three teaching hours

---

[1] For more details, please see http://www.law.tu.ac.th/en/courses-academic-programs.

per week for fifteen to sixteen weeks in a regular semester.

With regard to the total number of credits, the 141-credit program is very intensive which requires students to take a lot of courses in order to graduate. The courses contained within 141 credits can be categorized into the following groups.

1. General Education Courses   30 credits
2. Compulsory Courses   87 credits
3. Elective Courses   24 credits

As the country's oldest continuously operating law faculty, the law curriculum at Thammasat University Faculty of Law has become a model for Thai law schools established subsequently. Its law undergraduate curriculum is recognized by the Thai Bar Association as the standard Bachelor of Laws qualification for those who wish to be barristers. Thus, it is not surprised to see the similarity of law undergraduate curricula in Thailand.

However, such a curriculum is not supportive and presents a number of obstacles to law students who want to participate in an exchange program. In overall, Thammasat University has been a partner to many universities in terms of exchanging students between universities, but most of them focus on language study with the aim to improve skills in foreign languages. In the past, the Faculty of Law had inbound exchange students from Japan and the People's Republic of China who participated in our Thai-taught LL.B. program. Although they had some backgrounds in Thai language, it was still not easy for them to study laws in Thai language. On the other hand, we have seen very few students from Thai-taught program participating in an exchange program for legal study.

In the following section, we will discuss reasons why law students in Thai-taught program are not interested in joining international exchange program or collaboration.

3. Barriers Causing Problems to Students in Thai-taught LL.B. Program to Participate in an Exchange or Collaborative Program

3.1 Program Structure

The structure of Thai-taught LL.B. program is one of the obstacles for international exchange program or collaboration. The total number of credits required for graduation is 141 as mentioned earlier. The students are required to take 30 compulsory courses with the total of 87 credits. The distribution of those 30 compulsory courses in the four-year period is as follows.

Year	Number of compulsory courses
1st year	2 courses
2nd year	11 courses
3rd year	11 courses
4th year	6 courses

With the compulsory courses designed to be taken in each of the four years, students who participate in an exchange program or any collaboration will be behind their classmates in graduation. If they spend one semester or one year in an exchange program, it is very likely that they will not be able to graduate within four years. A student who wants to study abroad as an exchange student has to think hard whether the benefit to be gained from such a program would outweigh the loss from the delay of graduation. This is one of the reasons leading to the decision of not joining an exchange or collaborative program.

3.2 Transfer of Credits

As the Thai-taught LL.B. program was not originally designed to support an exchange program, the description of most courses in the curriculum is mainly focused on the contents of Thai law. Students who participate in an exchange program will find it difficult to have all credits from studying abroad transferred back to Thailand since the description of courses taken abroad does not match with that of courses in Thai-taught LL.B. program.

3.3 Modes of Assessment and the Scoring System

The Faculty of Law at Thammasat University has quite a unique method of assessment as compared with other faculties in Thammasat University. Each course has a total of 100 points. For the compulsory courses, they are assessed based on examination only. Most of the courses have only one final examination for the whole 100 points. Only a few courses have midterm examination. For elective courses, other modes of assessment are allowed such as report and presentation in classes.

With regard to the scoring system, Thammasat University Faculty of Law does not use the typical grading system, such as grades A, B, C. We have been using the scoring system which places the real score into the transcript. For example, if a student receives a score of 80 out of 100, the number "80" will be recorded on the transcript. This scoring system makes it difficult to match the letter grade obtained from studying abroad into the number of score to be appeared in the transcript.

3.4 Career Goal

Many students in Thai-taught LL.B. program have their goals on becoming judges or public prosecutors. Since the main language used in such careers is Thai, the students do not have any incentive to participate in any exchange program or collaboration. They do not want to spend one semester or one year abroad as they intend to study Thai law as much as possible and graduate so that they can prepare for the Bar examination and start their careers in those directions. To become a judge or public prosecutor, students have to take an examination for the admission of judge or public prosecutor. Although English is one of the subjects to be tested in such examinations, the proportion of the score is very small and therefore it does not draw the attention or give enough incentive for students to increase their English capability.

3.5 Language

The English language may be viewed as a problem in joining an exchange program since the students in Thai-taught LL.B. program uses Thai language most of the time. However, we have seen a lot of improvement in students' skills in English. Although they are students in Thai-taught program, but the English proficiency of many students nowadays are quite good. They should be able to use English effectively when they go to study abroad. Therefore, English skills may not be much of problem.

On the other side, it is obvious that language is a problem for students from foreign universities who want to come as inbound exchange students to study law in Thai-taught program at Thammasat University. Most classes are taught in Thai language which makes it virtually impossible for foreign students to understand.

We have presented a number of obstacles that do not give incentives to students in Thai-taught LL.B. program to participate in an exchange program or any collaboration. In the next section, we will discuss a new development that could encourage students in their decision to join an exchange program.

4. New Development to Increase the Incentives for Students in Thai-taught LL.B. Program on Participating in an Exchange or Collaborative Program

The Faculty of Law at Thammasat University is currently in the process of reforming its curriculum. The main idea in such a reform is to decrease the number of compulsory courses. The current program, as mentioned earlier, consists of 30 compulsory courses, which is considered to contain too many courses as compared to other universities around the world. We aim at decreasing the number of compulsory courses so that the students can have more freedom to choose elective courses that will lead them to specialization. They will also have time to improve skills in legal and language aspects outside the classroom.

In addition to the reduction of the number of compulsory courses, the study plan of the new reformed curriculum would be designed so that students can finish compulsory courses within the first three years. This plan would allow students to go to study abroad in the fourth year and transfer credits back into the transcript as earned credits at Thammasat University.

The grading system, to support the credit transfer, would be designed so that the courses from studying abroad to be transferred would be graded as "PASS", instead of the score or regular grade. It would eliminate the problem of the comparison between two different grading/scoring systems.

Furthermore, additional courses relating to foreign laws and comparative laws would be added into the new reformed curriculum. Such courses not only serve students' interests in the globalization era, they also provide an effective way to conduct the credit transfer for the students joining an exchange program. The course description would be more matched to the subject taken abroad. Moreover, the new reformed curriculum would be designed to have more courses offered in English language so that foreign students who want to join the exchange program as inbound students will be able to take such courses in English without any language difficulty.

In addition to all of the above features to be added into the new reformed curriculum, we can expect that more students would be interested in working in law firms or international organizations, which requires English for communication. The interests in those areas will give incentives for students in Thai-taught program to join an exchange program which will provide opportunities for students to gain legal knowledge outside Thailand as well as broaden their mind and vision towards the rapid change in the society.

5. Overview of Law Programs Taught in English Language at Thammasat University Faculty of Law

While the law curriculum of Thammasat University Faculty of Law has continually influenced the development of legal education in Thailand, we are also aware of the rapid change in social, economic and legal environments. The ASE-AN Economic Community is one example of imminent challenges to Thai legal education.

It is well recognized with regard to the need for lawyers capable of coping with complex business transactions involving international parties who use English as common language. In 2014, a new four-year undergraduate program entitled "the Bachelor of Laws Program in Business Law (International Program)" was launched at Thammasat University. This program is Thailand's only Bachelor of Laws program entirely taught in English. It presents an immense challenge for the legal educational system in a country where English is not an official language and where English publication on its law is rarely seen.

The English-taught LL.B. program requires at least 125 credits for graduation. The credits are categorized into groups as follows.

1. General Education Courses   30 credits
2. Compulsory Courses   41 credits
3. Elective Specialized (Law) Courses   48 credits
4. Elective Courses   6 credits

While the English-taught LL.B. program presents a challenging task for us, it also gives us good opportunities for exchange programs and various types of collaborations with other foreign universities. The reasons that this English-taught LL.B. program works in favor of exchange programs and collaborations can be described as follows.

(a) Language: As English is the language used entirely in the program, there is no difficulty in communication when the students from our international program go to study abroad. It also attracts foreign students who are interested in Thai law to come as inbound exchange students since all classes in this program are conducted in English.

(b) Structure of the program: The program is designed to have all compulsory courses completed at the end of the third year. This leaves the period of the fourth year available for students who want to go to study abroad. The students may choose to go to study abroad for one semester or even one full year.

(c) The transfer of credits: The program is designed to contain a number of courses whose contents are not necessarily Thai law. Examples of such courses include Business Law Seminar, Comparative Business Law, Comparative Private Law and Current Legal Issues as well as the Introduction of various Legal Systems such as American, English, Japanese, Chinese, French and German legal systems. Those courses will make it easier for the credit transfer. That is, when the students go to study abroad in an exchange program or any type of collaborations, the courses earned in foreign countries can be transferred back to those aforementioned courses in LL.B. program and counted as earned credits for graduation in Thailand.

(d) Assessments and the grading system: The English-taught LL.B. program implements various modes of assessments including class presentation, term paper, group project, midterm examination and final examination. Assessments will result in 8 levels of grades, namely, A, B+, B, C+, C, D+, D and F. This is the grading system typically used around the world, and it thus facilitates any exchange program and collaboration in terms of transfer of grade achieved from other universities.

(e) Main purpose of the program: The English-taught LL.B. program is designed to concentrate on the area of business law only. Thus, the students in this program have their main focus on becoming business lawyers. As the nature of business today inevitably involves with foreign and international components, the students would have strong incentives to learn foreign and international laws to gain advantages in their careers.

The English-taught LL.B. program is not the only program that is taught entirely in English. The Faculty of Law has also been operating another program entitled "the Master of Laws Program in Business Law (English Program)" since 2009. In this English-taught LL.M. program, the students have to study for a total of 39 credits in order to graduate with 15 of those credits being compulsory. The students may choose Plan A for thesis writing or Plan B for independent research. As the program is based on using English as communication language and the schedule of the program is quite flexible for students to join any exchange program or collaboration, this is also the program that we have seen a lot of positive activities towards cooperative relations with other foreign universities.

In the following section, we will discuss about existing exchange programs and collaborations in both LL.B. and LL.M. English-taught programs at Thammasat University Faculty of Law.

6. The Exchange Programs and Collaborations in English-taught Programs at Thammasat University Faculty of Law

We have so far seen a lot of progress and development on various types of collaborative activities in English-taught programs for both LL.B. and LL.M. The purpose of this section is to explore and study different models of collaborations. The names of partner universities will not be mentioned here as we only focus on the explanation of different types of collaborations.

According to the exchange programs and collaborations in legal study that we have with other universities, they can be categorized into four different models. The first two models are arranged for the English-taught LL.B. program while the last two models are set for the English-taught LL.M. program. The four models are explained as follows.

Model 1

This is the model for LL.B. students. This model is a real exchange program. It means that when we send one student from our program to the partner university, then the partner university will send one student to study with us in Thailand. The students joining this exchange program pay tuition fees at their own universities. This model has been operating and we have had inbound exchange students from many countries attending this program, such as Germany, France, The Netherlands, Finland and Canada. Our LL.B. students who join this model are usually the fourth-year students since there are no compulsory courses in the fourth year. The period that the students spend in the partner universities could be one semester or one full year, depending on the agreement.

The credits earned at the partner universities will be transferred back as the credits earned in the LL.B. program at Thammasat University, and can be used as a part of fulfillment for the LL.B. degree to be achieved at Thammasat University.

In summary, students joining the program in this model will spend the regular time (four years) to graduate from LL.B. at Thammasat University but they will have opportunities to gain knowledge and experience from studying abroad for one semester or one year.

Model 2

This is also the model for students in the LL.B. program. This model comes from a special agreement with our partner university. After our LL.B. students finish their third year at Thammasat University, they will spend one year at the partner university and earn an LL.M. degree at the partner university. The credits that are earned at the partner university can be transferred and counted as credits in LL.B. program at Thammasat University.

As for the LL.M. degree to be earned at the partner university, the students, at the end of their study at the partner university, have to show that they achieve the full credits at Thammasat University. The special advantage in this model is that the students can register and attend classes in LL.M. level at the partner university despite being only the fourth-year students. The challenge of this model is that the partner university has to allow our LL.B. students to start studying in LL.M. level even though they have not fulfilled all requirements at LL.B. level, provided that they will complete all credits for LL.B. (by the transfer of credits) at the end of the study in the partner university.

In summary, students joining the program in this model will spend four years and be able to achieve two degrees; one LL.B. from Thammasat University and one LL.M. from the partner university.

Model 3

This is the model implemented for English-taught LL.M. program. In this model, after our LL.M. students have finished the part of coursework at Thammasat University, they may spend one more year at one of our partner universities in order to achieve a degree in LL.M from the partner university. However, writing thesis is generally required when the students go to study at the partner universities.

For example, if an LL.M. student decides to go to a partner university, such a student will have to finish the coursework at Thammasat University first. Then, the student can choose whether he wants to finish the thesis as required at Thammasat University before or after he goes to study at a partner university. At the partner university, the student will have to take all courses and write a thesis within one year in order to complete an LL.M. degree abroad. The student has to complete all credits and fulfill all requirements from both Thammasat University and the partner university. Of course, at the end they will receive two degrees; one LL.M. from Thammasat University and another LL.M. from the partner university.

In summary, students will spend regular time in order to finish LL.M. at Thammasat University and will spend one more year at a partner university with the requirement on thesis writing. Special advantages that students may see from this model are the way that they can apply through the channel of relations between universities and the partner universities would give some special discounts on the tuition fee.

Model 4

This is also the model for students in LL.M. program. This model is derived from a special type of cooperative arrangement. In this model, our LL.M. students, while they are in Thailand, will take two courses that will be taught by professors from the partner university during summer semester in Thailand. It means that the Faculty of Law will invite professors from our partner university to come and teach for two courses. After the students finish such two courses, they are counted as parts of fulfillment at the partner university and the students will spend one more semester at the partner university and be able to graduate with an LL.M. degree at the partner university.

In summary, students will spend regular time in order to finish LL.M. at Thammasat University and will spend only one more semester at the partner university in order to achieve another LL.M abroad. This model is quite attractive and we have so far had about four to eight students a year participating in this program.

7. Conclusion

The student exchange programs and educational collaborations between universities can be used as potent ways to equip law students with knowledge and experience in foreign, international and comparative laws. It is also an important step to establish good relationship between universities, leading to future cooperation in other areas.

Thammasat University Faculty of Law has realized the significance of such programs and collaborations. The new reformed Thai-taught program and the launching of the English-taught LL.M. program in 2009 and the English-taught LL.B. program in 2014, as mentioned earlier in this paper, are good indications of our awareness and interests towards the law society that has increasing demand in lawyers equipped with foreign and international components of legal knowledge. We have witnessed positive progress and benefit achieved from such programs and collaborations to our students and students from our partner universities. We will continue our efforts to enhance our relationships with existing partners and seek additional relationships with other universities to promote mutual learning of knowledge and experience in legal community.

Chapter 6

INTERNATIONAL STUDENT EXCHANGE PROGRAMS FOR LEGAL EDUCATION AT UNIVERSITY OF YANGON

Khin Chit Chit*
(University of Yangon)

1. Introduction

Higher education is fundamental to a country's social and economic development. Higher education is responsible for nurturing skilled human capital needed in government, business and industry. Higher education institutions (HEIs) incubate creative thinking needed for an economically competitive society.

In order to sustain economic growth and compete in the global economy, Myanmar HEIs will be reformed to enable greater knowledge production and to develop highly skilled research centers that support social and economic development.[1] Myanmar has 158 higher education institutions (HEIs)(colleges, degree colleges and universities), which are overseen by 8 ministries.[2] Of those universities, the national University of Yangon is the oldest in Myanmar.

---

* Professor, Department of Law, University of Yangon.

[1] National Education Strategic Plan (2016-2021), Ministry of Education, Republic of Union of Myanmar, p.14

[2] Ibid, p.33

2. History of University of Yangon

The University of Yangon was established in December 1920 as the Rangoon University in accordance with the University of Rangoon Act (1920).

Although University status was granted in 1920, the Rangoon University existed before as the Rangoon College, founded in 1878, and affiliated to the University of Calcutta. The College was renamed Government College in 1904 and University College in 1920, when University College (Rangoon College-secular) and Judson College (Baptist-affiliated) were merged by the University of Rangoon Act (1920).

3. Vision for the University of Yangon

The University of Yangon is to be the leading higher educational institution in Myanmar and a Flagship University on par with regional counterparts and in line with international trends.

Today University of Yangon aims to be a flagship university of Myanmar, in accordance with Article 26 of the National Education Law (2014) enacted on 30 September 2014. To be a flagship university, UY faces many challenges such as the need for capacity building, an improved academic environment and international co-operation.

4. Legal Education in University of Yangon

Legal education in Myanmar started at University of Rangoon (today's University of Yangon) in 1920. The Law Department then offered a Law Degree known as Bachelor of Laws (BL), which was a part time post graduate degree. The BL degree required a two year course of study. The BL courses were fully taught in English. In 1965, a new system of higher education brought about a five-year fulltime legal education course for BA (Law) LLB degree at the Law Department, University of Yangon (UY). Myanmar language became the medium of instruction for teaching and learning of all the courses. Students were awarded a BA (Law) degree after 4 years of study and had to continue their studies one more year to receive the LLB. The LLM program was started in 1973 at the Law Department.

In 1976, a new higher education system was introduced in Myanmar. The system meant that students had to attend three years fulltime legal education after studying two years at the Regional Colleges for the LLB degree. Myanmar language was the medium of instruction for teaching and learning of all the courses. In 1982, a five-year fulltime legal education course was reintroduced for the LLB degree at the Law Department, University of Yangon. In 1987, English language was reintroduced as a medium of instruction for teaching and learning. From 1996 to 2013, the Department of Law, University of Yangon was only offering post graduate legal studies. University of Yangon has been a postgraduate only institution from 1996. In 1999, the PhD program was started at the Law Department, University of Yangon.

In 2013, undergraduate law courses were made available again for outstanding students who obtained a high score in the BEHS examination. Moreover, the Department of Law, University of Yangon offered 9 months Diplomas in four different areas of Law: Business Law, International Law, Maritime Law and Intellectual Property Law. A two years long MA program in Business Law was also offered.

5. Requirement for Improvement of Legal Education

Legal education is a vital component of a working legal system. Like breathing life into machine, legal education gives life to formal legal institutions by characterizing the functions and features of the national legal system.[3] There-

---

[3] Comparative Legal Education from Asian Perspective, "Why and How should comparative

fore, the improvement of legal education is very important not only for developed countries, but also for developing countries. In Myanmar, most graduate students require professional skills to enter the job market. The current legal education needs to be reformed to remain in touch with actual legal practice. To improve legal education problems around insufficient human resources, capacity, academic environment and international co-operation need to be addressed.

6. International Collaboration and Development Partners

The necessity of legal assistance from one country to another is an unavoidable reality of this 21st century's human society. Collaboration in legal education is important for the improvement of legal education. Professors and experts from foreign universities have visited the Department of Law, University of Yangon to give special lectures and hold seminars for undergraduate and post graduate students, as well as teaching staff, to improve the capacity for the different fields of law since 2013. As for Japan, the Myanmar Japan Legal Research Center was established and series of seminars on different areas of laws are conducted by this Center. International collaboration and development partners of Law Department, UY are

- ➢ Open Society Foundations
- ➢ Nagoya University, School of Law, Japan
- ➢ Australian National University, Australia
- ➢ University of Oxford, UK
- ➢ Columbia University, US
- ➢ National University of Singapore (NUS)Faculty of Law
- ➢ Central European University, Hungary
- ➢ Chuo University, Japan

Legal Education be promoted in an Asian Context?" written by Hiroshi Matsuo, Edited by KEIGLAD, Keio Institute for Global Law and Department, Keio University, Japan, Pg 3

- Singapore Management University (SMU) Law School
- University of Toulouse I, France and
- UNDP partnering BABSEA CLE (Bridges Across Borders Southeast Asia Community Legal Education Initiative) (Valid data as of 26 September 2017)

7. Current Students at Law Department (2016-2017) Academic Year

The number of students at Law Department for the 2016-2017 Academic Year are as follows;

- First Year LLB................... 110
- Second Year LLB 48
- Third Year LLB....................37
- Fourth Year LLB 50
- First Year Master.................23
- Second Year Master 24
- MRes 13
- PhD Preliminary Course.....23
- Thesis (First Year)...............21
- Thesis (Second Year)...........27
- Thesis (Third Year) 19
- Thesis (Final Year)................8

8. International Student Exchange Programs

University of Yangon is encouraging international exchange of both students and teachers. An effective way to implement the exchange between students and teachers of the University of Yangon is to enter into MOU or MOA.

Studying abroad opportunities for students increased in 2015, in UY. Most students involved in study abroad are at College or University. A well-designed program combines academic learning, socio-cultural experiences, sightseeing and sometimes community services. As for the Law Department, one first year master student was selected to participate in the Japan-East Asia Network of Exchange for Students and Youths which was sponsored by the Japanese Government in 2015. She was given the opportunity to study at Tokyo Women Colleges. Since 2015, 18 students from the Law Department have been given the chance to study abroad (short term/long term program). Eight students had the chance to study in Japan; such as at the Tokyo Women Colleges, Waseda University and Musashino University, Josai University, Nagoya University and Keio University. In addition, four students participated to the Rule of Law and Sustainable Development Workshop in the Thailand Institute of Justice. One student received a scholarship to attend Law studies at Manchester University, England. One student attended the ASEAN Intergovernmental Commission Human Rights 2015 at National University of Singapore. Two students studied at Busan University, Korea and two students had the opportunity to participate to the IHL Moot Court competition in Hong Kong. For most of the students who went abroad, this was the very first time they left Myanmar. But many students cannot be given the opportunity to participate in international students exchange programs. Increased participation is needed, to enable foreign exposure and improvement. Students who are able to participate derive a lot of benefits but also face many challenges.

9. Benefits of International Student Exchange Programs

a. Increased Self-confidence

International students on an International Student Exchange Programs have to leave their home and explore a foreign country totally unknown to them. They also learn to adapt to unfamiliar surroundings and living conditions. As a result, they become bolder and more confident.

b. Improved Academic Performance & Experience from Learning Difficulties

Students have a chance to experience different teaching and different assessments methods applied in another university.

c. Greater Understanding of One's own Cultural Values

Students who live abroad for an exchange program learn to appreciate the different culture of their host country. They develop a better understanding and appreciation for the nation's people and history. They also bring their own culture with them. As a result, their hosts can learn about and become familiar with that culture.

d. Opportunity to Study Foreign Language

Studying abroad grants the students the opportunity to completely immense themselves in a new language. There is no better way to learn.

e. Improve Career Prospects

Student exchange programs improve the career prospect of participants. Because of their access to broader perspectives and their exposure to international communities, they can be sought after by companies that operate in different parts of the world.

f. Life Experience

Students can access opportunities to travel abroad for a long time. Eventually they can find a good job and career. The opportunity to study abroad may turn out to be a once in a life time experience.

g. Foreign Exposure

Students can access the chance to participate in discussions, workshops and presentations in a foreign country.

10. Challenges to International Student Exchange Programs

Despite the advantages of international education, international students encounter a wide range of issues when they live and study abroad. Those issues are generally related to language difficulties, adaptation to a new learning system, psychological problems such as homesickness, discrimination, and feeling isolated. Socio-cultural problems in relation to health care and financial systems are also experienced. Other issues include financial difficulties, depression, and culture shock.

a. Language Issues

Language difficulties seem to be the one of challenging issues experienced by international students. For example. Filling forms for registration at the University was difficult for foreign students difficult as they were written in Japanese; but teachers and staffs translated for them. All students can access the paper and machine (computers, photocopying machines?) for free at the University. This meant they had to do all these things by themselves. Only the Japanese font is installed on every computer at University. So student who wants to print out or copy paper, face a language problem.

b. Adaptation to a New Learning and Assessments System

In Myanmar, final exams are done in exam rooms. In Japan, final exams are not done in exam room. Students have to submit reports and make presentations as mid-term exams and final exams.

c. Differences in Culture and Practices (Culture Shock)

Students encounter a range of socio-cultural barriers and social issues. International students face difficulty in forming new friendships with local citizens due to cultural differences and language barriers.

d. Financial Issues

Important issues for international students are insufficient funding and currency differences. They may also face basic welfare issues. As Myanmar currency is lower than Japanese currency, prices are higher and things are expensive for Myanmar students. Insufficient funds has led some international students to give depression.

e. Academic Credit Transfer

The main challenge to for credit transfer and accompanying student mobility in Asian nations seems to be harmonizing of the existing higher education systems. Therefore, it is better to harmonize and work with existing systems rather than to create a new one.

f. Different Academic Calendars

A rigid curriculum makes credit transfer difficult for students who participate in mobility programs. The existence of two different academic calendars in Asian states also present an important difficulty for mobility within as well as outside the region. In order to foster mobility universities in the region will have to move towards a more international academic calendar: September to December, and February to early June. This will make the academic calendar compatible for the Asian region.

11. Conclusion

To help reduce these difficulties, policy makers, faculty members, and counselors should expand effort to meet international student needs and address the particular issues of international students, particularly those involving work, government relationships, social integration, and language support. Also, academic higher institutions and hosting countries should collaborate to increase international students' awareness of host countries' society and help international students to integrate and contribute to these societies.

Chapter 7

COMPARATIVE LEGAL EDUCATION:

Challenges for Studying Law Abroad

Khin Phone Myint Kyu*

(University of Yangon)

1. Introduction

A legal education is the study of principles, practices, and theories of law. In Myanmar, we can study the law in two ways. First, is the pursuit of a LL.B. degree for on-campus students, and the second is enrollment in distance learning courses. Sixteen Departments in different areas of Myanmar are on-campus teaching Universities and another two are distance teaching Universities in different area of Myanmar.

Academic staff exchange programs play an important role in enhancing the capacity, not only of the teachers but also of the students. To implement this program, we need to sign Memoranda of Understanding (MoU) or Memoranda of Agreement (MoA) with partner universities. Before signing a MoU or the MoA, we need to negotiate thoroughly and set the terms of the agreement.

---

* Professor, Department of Law, University of Yangon, Myanmar.

– 93 –

2. Facts about the University of Yangon

The University of Yangon was established on December 1, 1920. Thus, it is the oldest national university in Myanmar. There are twenty-one academic departments, each headed by a professor. Thirteen departments are for the arts, namely the Anthropology, Archaeology, English, Geography, History, International Relations, Law, Library and Information Studies, Myanmar, Oriental Studies, Philosophy, Political Science, and Psychology Departments. The remaining eight are science departments, namely the Botany, Chemistry, Computer Science, Geology, Industrial Chemistry, Mathematics, Physics, and Zoology Departments.

Since University of Yangon is now an institution for undergraduate and postgraduate studies, offering B.A. or B.A. (Honours), B.Sc. or B.Sc. (Honours), LL.B., Post-graduate Diploma, M.A., M.Sc., LL.M., MRes, and Ph.D. degrees. In the coming academic year, however, the University will no longer offer the MRes degree.

Each academic year consists of two semesters. The first semester begins in December and ends in March and the second semester begins in June and ends in September.

The University of Yangon composes of one rector, two pro-rectors, fifty-two professors, thirty-nine associate professors, three hundred and eighty lecturers, two hundred and thirty-nine assistant lecturers, and one hundred and twenty-one tutors and demonstrators. There are an additional five hundred and fifty administrative staff members in our University.[1] In the Department of Law, there are four professors, fourteen lecturers, eight assistant lecturers, and two tutors. There are no associate professors in the Department of Law.

---

[1] Data as of September, 2017.

COMPARATIVE LEGAL EDUCATION

3. Human Resource Development Program (HRD) in University of Yangon

Since 1998, the University of Yangon has implemented the HRD Program. Under this program, the University of Yangon provides Diploma Courses in computer science, geology, international relations, law, oriental studies, geography, and history to help to develop the skills and education of the technicians and intellectuals needed in the community. Aside from these HRD Diploma Courses, the University also provides HRD Master's Degrees in computer science (web-based teaching systems) and business law.

The Post-Graduate Diploma Program has been offered by the Department of Law under the HRD Program since 2004. The Department has four diploma courses; these are the Diploma in Business Law, International Law, Maritime Law, and Intellectual Property Law. These are offered as part-time courses in the early morning, 7:00 am to 9:00 am. Any graduate is entitled to attend in these diploma courses, but they must sit for the entrance exam. These diploma courses last one year (two semesters).

Moreover, our department offers a Master of Arts in Business Law under the HRD Program. This is full-time course and lasts two years (four semesters). In order to attend this master's course, it is necessary to have graduate diploma in business law and pass an entrance examination.

4. Regular Programs of Study at the University of Yangon

The University of Yangon initiated doctorate courses in the 1994–1995 Academic Year. However, the Department of Law started to offer a five-year Ph.D. program in 1999. The first year is devoted to studying preliminary theory and the last four years are devoted to the preparation of a candidate's dissertation.

The Department of Law also provides LL.B., LL.M., and MRes. degrees. At the master's level, the Department of Law offers four specializations: the Civil

Law Specialization, International Law Specialization, Maritime Law Specialization, and Commercial Law Specialization. We can accept ten candidates for each specialization each academic year.

5. International Collaboration for Capacity Building

The University of Yangon has two international collaboration programs for capacity building. One is visiting fellow program, and the other is long-term collaboration program.

Under the visiting fellow program, the university participates in a scholar exchanges in the International Relations, Law, and Archaeology Departments, supported by Open Society Foundations (OSF), and the Visiting Professor Program through the ASEAN University Network-Southeast Asia Engineering Education Development Network (AUN-SEED/Net) Program. In 2014, our university has established an e-Library with the support of OSF.

For the long-term collaboration program, the University entered the ASEAN University Network (AUN) in 2012. Through this network, the University is conducting AUN-QA training and implementation and a AUN/SEED-Net Scholarship Program. The University of Yangon is collaborating with Chung Ang University, Korea; Hanyang University, Korea; Nagoya University, Japan; and Cologne University, Germany. Among these, the Department of Law has collaborated with Nagoya University.

The University of Yangon has signed fifty four agreements, MoUs and MoAs, with international institutions and foreign universities.[2]

In order to enter into one of these agreements, a foreign university needs to send proposal to sign a MoU or MoA to the University of Yangon. After receiving the proposal, the University of Yangon submits it to our University Senate, accompanied with the suggestion of the Department of Law. It is then submitted

---

[2] Appendix I

to the Ministry of Education through the Department of Higher Education for their permission. During this process, the proposal is also assessed by the MoU and MoA Assessment Board, and then the two universities can negotiate, according to the assessment of said Board. After receiving permission, we can hold the signing ceremony. This is a very long process.

Since the University of Yangon is a government financed university, all of the teaching staff are civil servants. Therefore, the teaching staff who want to study law cannot go abroad without permission. The application process to receive permission is not easy because it has many steps and takes a long time.

First, it is necessary to receive an official invitation letter for the respective participant to attend a seminar, workshop, or master's or Ph.D. course to the respective participant through the Myanmar Embassy in the foreign country. After receiving the invitation letter, the candidate must apply through a bureaucratic channel to receive permission from the Myanmar government. The application procedure takes about two months. The candidate applies to University Senate to gain the approval of the senators. If all of the senators agree, the application submitted to the Ministry of Education and the Cabinet through the Department of Higher Education (Lower/Upper Myanmar Branch). After receiving permission, the candidate applies for a deputation order, an official passport, and a visa. Even if a candidate already has an official passport, it is necessary to renew it.

If a foreigner from collaborating university wants to study at the University of Yangon, he must send an offer letter with his curricular vitae, a copy of passport, and a recommendation letter through the relevant university and academic department. The relevant department must apply for him through the Senate to the Ministry of Education to receive permission. After permission is granted, the University of Yangon sends invitation letter to the applicant.

6. International Exchange Program for Legal Education

In order to implement the international exchange program for legal education, not only for teaching staff but also for students, it is necessary to sign a Memorandum of Understanding (MoU) or Memorandum of Agreement (MoA) between the University of Yangon and the foreign university. If there is a MoU or MoA between the two universities, it will be easier to carry out the exchange program.

The University of Yangon has already collaborated with many foreign universities under MoUs for student exchange programs and foreign lectures. Under the MoUs between University of Yangon and (1) Nagoya University, (2) the National University of Singapore Faculty of Law and Singapore Management University School of Law, (3) Bridges Across Borders Southeast Asia Community Legal Education (BABSEA CLE), and (4) Chuo University, the Department of Law is conducting student exchange programs.

The Department of Law of the University of Yangon received one student from Chuo University for an academic year and sent two law students to Nagoya University for six months. Even though the University of Yangon has experience in student exchange, no legal teaching staff have participated in long-term exchanges (a semester or longer).

Under the MoU with Nagoya University, the Myanmar-Japan Legal Research Center was established on the University of Yangon campus. A series of seminars on different areas of law are conducted by the Center and Japanese Law Professors give lectures on different subjects. Furthermore, many law professors from different foreign universities (such as Australia National University, National University of Singapore, Central European University, and Colombia University) have visited our Department and provided training, seminars, workshops, and lectures to improve the capacity of the teaching staff in particular fields of law. Most of the training is on the topic of international human rights law, comparative constitutional law, international law, international environmental law, rule of law, and law of contracts. Besides these training opportunities, both the centre and foreign teachers gave special training to upgrade the curriculum design. The Clinical Legal Education (CLE) program sponsored by the United Nations Development Programme (UNDP) provided training for teaching staff, not only to improve legal education but also to have an opportunity to learn new teaching methods. The CLE program provided the opportunity for teaching staff to attend a pro bono workshop and other trainings held in different foreign countries. Thus, many teaching staff can receive not only training and experience but also foreign exposure.

Although we do not have a long-term teaching staff exchange program, many foreign universities, such as Columbia University in the United States, the University de Toulouse in France, Oxford University in the United Kingdom, the Central European University, the Australian National University, the National University of Singapore, Singapore Management University, Nagoya University in Japan, and Ho Chi Minh University in Vietnam have invited the teaching staff to make presentations and provide special lectures related to Myanmar law and legal education in Myanmar. Moreover, young teaching staff can receive scholarships in foreign universities for a master's or doctoral degree.

Teaching staff exchange programs and scholarship programs provide not only a cultural learning experience but also provide the means for expanding and enriching a teacher's pedagogical expertise. Moreover, teaching staff can learn about different classroom cultures and teaching methodologies, such as role play, short presentations, and small group discussions. Furthermore, they can learn how to manage their lecture time by using effective teaching methods. When they return to their Departments, they can share their experience with their students and colleagues.

7. Problems and Obstacles for Further Development of International Exchange Programs

Most of the scholarship program invitations arrive in the hands of candidates the day before the deadline, and sometimes even on or after the deadline. So, it is necessary to send them as early as possible because of the long application procedure.

We can find scholarship programs from university websites. But, if Myanmar teaching staff tried independently to apply for a scholarship program on a website, it will take more time and raise more challenges to gain permission. Because it is out of the proper channel.

8. Conclusion

Staff exchange programs have been properly developed in the course of Myanmar language, and it is still an ongoing process. However, for the legal field, there is no established practice for staff exchange.

It is necessary to initiate a staff exchange program for the legal field. In order to implement a staff exchange program effectively, it is necessary for universities to sign MOU/MOAs.

Appendix I

List of Agreements and MoUs with International Institutions and Foreign Universities:

1. Cologne University, Germany (2003)
2. Thepsatri Rajabhat University, Thailand (4/9/2013)
3. Hankuk University of Foreign Studies, Korea (5/3/2013)
4. Korea Foundation for Advanced Studies (6/13/2013)
5. Nagoya University, Japan (6/29/2013)
6. Australia National University (9/9/2013)
7. National University of Singapore Faculty of Law and Singapore Management University School of Law (2/18/2014)
8. Chonnam National University, Korea (2/24/2014)
9. Korea Research Institute of Bioscience and Biotechnology (2/25/ 2014)
10. Hanyang University, Korea (2/27/2014)

COMPARATIVE LEGAL EDUCATION

11. Yunnam Normal University, China (6/5/2014)

12. Passau University, Germany (6/14/2014)

13. Oxford University, United Kingdom (7/15/2014)

14. Tokyo University of Foreign Studies, Japan (8/6/2014)

15. Bridges Across Borders Southeast Asia Community Legal Education (BABSEA CLE) (8/12/2014)

16. Chung-Ang University, Korea (8/15/2014)

17. United Overseas Bank, Singapore (8/28/2014)

18. Akita University, Japan (8/19/2014)

19. Kansai University of International Studies, Japan (10/28/2014)

20. Jeju National University, Korea (11/7/2014)

21. Beijing Foreign Studies University, China (1/14/2015)

22. Srinakharinwirot University, Thailand (1/28/2015)

23. Kokushikan University, Japan (2/27/2015)

24. University of Wollongong, Australia (3/6/2015)

25. Chuo University, Japan (3/19/2015)

26. Chiang Mai University, Thailand (4/24/2015)

27. National Institute of Medicinal Materials (NIMM), Vietnam (5/8/2015)

28. Waseda University, Japan (5/14/2015)

29. Busan University of Foreign Studies, Korea (5/27/2015)

30. Osaka University, Japan (6/18/2015)

31. Tokyo University of Marine Science and Technology, Japan (7/1/2015)

32. Yunnan Minzu University, China (7/3/2015)

33. Chung Yuan Christian University, Taiwan (7/8/2015)

34. National Pingtun University of Science and Technology, Taiwan (7/8/2015)

35. POSCO TJ Park Foundation, Korea (7/21/2015)

36. Southern Taiwan University of Science and Technology (8/7/2015)

37. Chinese Culture University, Taiwan (8/5/2015)

38. Feng Chia University, Taiwan (8/7/2015)

39. National Taiwan Ocean University (8/14/2015)

40. Josai University Corporation, Japan (8/25/2015)

41. School of Chemical & Life Sciences Nanyang Polytechnic (9/1/2015)

42. Norway David Taw Scholarship Fund Programme (9/4/2015)

43. Oslo and Akershus University College of Applied Science, Faculty of Social Sciences, Norway (9/10/2015)

44. Kyushu University, Japan (9/18/2015)

45. Kyoto University, Japan (9/22/2015)

46. Osaka University of Economics and Law, Japan (7/8/2015)

47. Guangdong University of Foreign Studies, China (1/20/2016)

48. Zeppelin University, Germany (2/29/2016)

49. Central European University, Hungary (4/3/2016)

50. The Institute of Geography and Geology at ERNST-MORITZ-ARNDT-University Greifswald, Germany (2/5/16)

51. National Taipei University, Taiwan (6/6/16)

52. Midwest University, American (6/17/16)

53. National Chi Nan University, Taiwan (7/4/16)

54. Baoshan University, China (6/27/16)

Chapter 8

GLOBALIZING
JAPANESE LEGAL EDUCATION
AT KEIO UNIVERSITY LAW SCHOOL ("KLS"):

Exchange and Double Degree Arrangements as One Arrow in the Quiver

David G. Litt*

(Keio University)

1. Introduction

Japanese universities, supported by the Japanese education bureaucracy, recognize a need to "globalize" further in order to achieve a number of different objectives. Different objectives may require different methods, and may rest upon varying interpretations of the term "globalize". The objectives include:

- To better prepare students for a world in which they will need to function across borders and cultures.

- To better meet companies' and other employers' needs for future staff in order to compete and prosper in a globalized economy.

- To elevate the global profiles (and, inevitably, rankings) of top Japanese universities as one method to retain the best researchers and attract funding, so that Japanese universities can be leading global centers of research and teaching in many fields.

---

* Professor of Law, Keio University Law School.

– 103 –

2. The 2004 Legal Education Reform and the Japanese Law School System

As others have described, Japan launched its new law schools and reform of the legal education and qualification system in 2004.[1] The reform was intended to produce a legal profession better able to meet the needs of business and society, and to attract larger numbers of talented individuals into the profession, including individuals who had studied other subjects as undergraduates, and who had even worked in different fields before entering law school.

The 2004 reform, as implemented, is often viewed critically. Many more law schools than were needed—74 law schools in all—opened their doors. Fewer than half that number would have sufficed. To make matters worse, the reform was designed in an environment of rapidly expanding demand for all kinds of legal services, but the first classes of the new *Juris Doctor* (JD) program graduates entered the job market just at the start of the global financial crisis, as demand for new lawyers in Japan, the United States and much of Europe fell more than at any time in the prior twenty-five years.

Even those students who successfully completed a JD program and passed the bar exam faced weak employment prospects for a number of years during and after the global financial crisis. The 2004 reform had initially been planned with a target eventually to produce 3000 new legal professionals—lawyers, judges and prosecutors—each year. But the number never exceeded 2500, and was cut back by 2016 to its current level of just over 1500 successful bar exam takers per year.[2]

Needless to say, with too many schools, too many graduates, and a lower

---

[1] For a description of the Japanese legal education and bar qualification system up to the 2004 reform, see Kahei Rokumoto, *Legal Education*, in Daniele H. Foote ed., *Law in Japan: a turning point*, University of Washington Press, 2007, Chapter 8, pp. 191-232.

[2] For an excellent discussion of the implementation of the 2004 reform and its near-term results, see Daniele H. Foote, "The Trials and Tribulations of Japan's Legal Education Reform," *Hastings International & Comparative Law Review*, Volume 36, 2013, pp. 369-442.

than anticipated cap on successful bar exam takers, many students' hopes were disappointed, as the bar passage rate eventually fell into the 20-25% range, far below the "U.S.-style" bar exam with a 75% passage rate that had been anticipated when the system was planned.

In Japan, in order to sit for the national bar exam an individual must have either received a JD from one of the Japanese law schools or passed a special preliminary exam (known in Japanese as the "*yobi shiken*"). Over 95% of those sitting for the bar each year have gone the JD route. But the *yobi shiken* is a very good predictor of success on the bar exam, so the bar exam passage rate is much higher for those who qualify to sit for the bar based upon the *yobi shiken*, and such applicants exceed 10% of total successful bar applicants in recent years.

As a result of the low overall bar exam passage rate, most JD students at Japanese law schools focus their effort upon preparation for the bar exam, more than on acquiring knowledge and skills that will serve them best in legal practice. And despite the 2004 reform, most law students and new lawyers today do not have degrees in other subjects as undergraduates, nor work experience. As before 2004, most study law as undergraduates. And most go to law school directly after completing an undergraduate program or, if they pass the *yobi shiken*, even skip or withdraw from a JD program.

Despite these continuing concerns, in 2017, over a decade after the first JD class graduated, we can see many positive benefits of the 2004 reform, including

- A much larger and more diverse bar of practicing lawyers;
- a new, large group of professionally trained in-house lawyers working within Japanese corporations;
- many lawyers working within Japanese government agencies; and
- a greater ability of the Japanese bar to meet needs of consumers of legal services across the entire spectrum, from individuals' need for basic, affordable legal services to businesses' need for advice and implementation of extremely complex transactions.

Similarly, now that almost half of the law schools launched in 2004 have closed their doors, the legal education system is much closer to the "right size" to meet the needs of its various constituencies.

And one of many benefits of the post-2004 reform system is the opportunity for more international, globally relevant education.

3. Keio University Law School ("KLS") Programs

KLS offers a variety of international programs, aimed at a number of different student constituencies. I will focus on the programs and exchange opportunities that KLS offers with instruction in English language.

We have two groups of degree students at KLS, and also various non-degree students, whom these programs serve.

3.1 KLS JD Program

The JD program at Keio includes a 3-year course, which is the standard requirement, and a 2-year course for those who have studied law as undergraduates (receiving an LL.B. or equivalent) and passed a placement test. In fact, the 2-year course is now much more popular than the 3-year one. There are just under 200 students per class year in the KLS JD program.

As noted above, a Japanese law school program is designed to prepare students to become legal professionals in Japan—lawyers, judges and prosecutors. KLS graduates included 152 successful bar exam takers in 2016, and 144 in 2017. In both these years, KLS had more successful bar exam takers than any other law school in Japan. Typically in recent years, between 45 and 50 percent of KLS graduates who sit for the bar exam will pass each year, and graduates may sit for the exam up to three years. The passage rate is much higher for those with high grades/GPAs, for those who studied law as undergraduates and then completed the 2-year JD course, and for first-time exam takers.

3.2 KLS LL.M. in Global Legal Practice

In April, 2017, KLS added a second program, the LL.M. in Global Legal

Practice. This program is outlined by Prof. Rikako Watai in the previous volume in this series.[3]

In its second semester of operation Fall term of 2017, the LL.M. program now has 25 students, and its eventual target is 30. Of the current students, 8 are Japanese and 17 non-Japanese. The non-Japanese are mostly practicing attorneys, and come from many countries, among others: Brazil, China, France, Germany, Kenya, Singapore, Switzerland, Thailand, the United States, and Vietnam). The LL.M. is designed so that it can be completed in one academic year. Students who attend the program part-time while working will typically require longer (1.5 or 2 years, or longer). In April, 2018, the LL.M. program will implement Certificates in Business Law, International Dispute Resolution, and Japanese Law, as discussed below.

3.3 Keio Non-KLS Programs in Law

KLS was set up in 2004 as a new professional school, but Keio University retains other significant law-focused programs.

Keio maintains a Faculty of Law, which continues to offer a very large and popular LL.B. program for undergraduates. The first two years of this program are taught at the Hiyoshi Campus, in between Tokyo and central Yokohama, while the latter two years are at the Mita Campus in central Tokyo, where KLS is located.

In addition to the graduate programs at KLS, Keio maintains a Graduate School of Law. The Graduate School of Law continues to offer Master and Ph.D. programs for those who pursue law as an academic subject, while KLS focuses on professional training for practitioners.

The faculty, organizations and programs of KLS and the Graduate School of Law are distinct, though there is a great deal of overlap, including many KLS

---

[3] R. Watai, *Current Status of Legal Education in Japan*, in Keio Institute for Global Law and Development (KEIGLAD) ed., *Comparative Legal Education from Asian Perspective*, 2017, pp. 131-142.

professors who teach classes in the Faculty of Law or Graduate School of Law, and Faculty of Law/Graduate School of Law professors who also teach classes at KLS.[4]

Finally, Keio has other programs that overlap significantly with what might, in some other countries, fall within a law school. An example is Keio's Faculty of Policy Management, which focuses on inter-disciplinary study of public policy but includes much study of law and regulation.

3.4 Inbound Exchange Students

Inbound exchange students are another important group for KLS' English language law offerings. Typically, we host 10 to 20 exchange students from around the globe each term studying at KLS. The number is slightly larger in the fall than spring. In the Fall of 2017, we are hosting 20 exchange students at KLS. A list of law schools with which KLS has exchange agreements in place is set forth below at Table 1.

3.4.1 Types of In-Bound Exchanges to Keio

Some exchange students come for a semester and others for a full year. While at KLS, many of these students also study Japanese language intensively, taking advantage of Keio's university-wide Japanese language training offerings for exchange and other international students.

We also offer some short-term inbound exchanges, especially under the PAGLEP arrangements. These include several students who have come for short term exchange in advance of a semester, or for internships, or as part of a group to participate in a concentrated course on a topic of interest.

---

[4] For law schools located within private universities in Japan, this structure of a separate (1) law school and (2) faculty of law/graduate school of law, is typical. It is based upon compliance with government regulations for the law schools. Thus, when law schools within private universities have closed down in Japan, typically the university continues to maintain a faculty of law program for undergraduates and, in many cases, a graduate school of law for master's and Ph.D. candidates.

GLOBALIZING JAPANESE LEGAL EDUCATION AT KEIO UNIVERSITY LAW SCHOOL ("KLS")

Table 1

KLS Cooperation Agreements (non-PAGLEP)

(Most but not all these agreements include student exchange)

Cornell University
Georgetown University
The College of William and Mary
University of California, Los Angeles
University of Illinois
University of Auckland
University of British Columbia
Sciences Po
Panthéon-Assas Paris II University
Ewha Womans University
Yonsei University
Sogang University
Chonnam National University
University of Zurich
The University Paris 13
Humboldt-Universität zu Berlin
Chung-Ang University
University of Malta
University of Washington
Sungkyunkwan University
Tsinghua University
National Taiwan University
Singapore Management University
Freiburg University
City University London
Universität Hamburg, Fakultät für Rechts-wissenschaft
University of Washington School of Law
Seoul National University School of Law
Université Libre de Bruxelles

Also there many Keio university-wide cooperation and exchange agreements that include KLS potentially. (For example: Melbourne University has an agreement with Keio which could potentially include law school students from both institutions). Keio overall has exchange students from nearly 70 countries.

– 109 –

3.4.2 Why does Keio support so many in-bound exchanges?

Typically KLS exchange agreements provide for "balance" of inbound and outbound students, and mutual waiver of tuition at the "host" school. This allows students to go on exchange without worry of different tuition levels, and is the global standard for these kinds of arrangements.

In the case of KLS, however, as noted below, there are many, many more inbound exchanges than outbound. Thus, KLS is in essence offering "free" education for a number of students coming to Japan on exchange. While there are limits to the extent of imbalance that can be sustained, there are good reasons to at least allow some excess and to welcome inbound students.

First, the exchange relationship builds a long-term network for collaboration at all levels, in and outside of the university. These create rich opportunities for outbound exchanges, and in many cases, all a Keio student or faculty member needs to do is to ask in order to take advantage of one of these.

Second, the presence of very strong exchange students from many of the best universities around the globe can assist in globalization of Japan and of Keio University, as the exchange students participate in Keio programs of many types together with Japanese students.

The exchange students who come to KLS often form long-term engagement with Japan, in which Keio plays an important part. There are former KLS exchange students now working in many law firms and companies in Tokyo, and, indeed, teaching courses at KLS on topics related to business law, mergers & acquisitions, and international dispute resolution. Even when inbound students do not remain in, or return to, Japan, many have a lasting engagement working with Japanese companies, colleagues or collaborators back in their home countries.

3.5 Recurrent Education

Many KLS international subjects taught in English are open to limited numbers of practicing attorneys for "recurrent" (or "continuing") legal education.

The recurrent "monitor" program allows Japanese lawyers who did not take advantage of English language, international, elective courses while in law school to do so later on. These students are typically in law firms or corporate legal departments and find themselves in need of the skill training that KLS offers, and we are delighted to include them in order to better serve the needs of the Japanese legal profession. We also find that having experienced practitioners in the classroom can add significantly to discussion of legal practice.

3.6 Typical Class Composition

Thus, a typical class taught at KLS with instruction in English in the Fall term of 2017 might have:

- 10 to 12 LL.M. students, perhaps 4 Japanese and 6 to 8 non-Japanese, many of whom are practictioners;
- 8 graduate-level exchange students from law schools such as Georgetown, UCLA and Cornell (U.S.A), University of British Columbia (Canada), Humboldt University Berlin (Germany), University of Zurich (Switzerland), Tsinghua (Beijing), and Hanoi (Vietnam);
- 4 KLS JD students, all Japanese; and
- 5 "recurrent" students who are practicing Japanese lawyers.

We can thus offer a very international classroom, with students from many countries and with a range of practical experience.

4. Out-bound Exchanges from Keio

4.1 KLS JD Student Outbound Exchanges

Almost all KLS JD students are reluctant to go on semester-length exchanges. Since the bar exam in Japan is given only once each year, and they cannot easily complete enough courses while on exchange to stay "on track" for the JD program in Japan, an overseas exchange typically extends their JD education by one or two semesters and delays their bar exam by a year.

Employers in Japan seem to place an emphasis on students who get through the educational system and bar exam quickly, so students perceive delay as not only costing them time and money, but also potentially hurting their immediate post-graduation career prospects.

4.1.1 Semester and Full-Year Abroad

Some students, however, do take longer exchanges. To give a few examples:

This year we have one JD student on exchange for a term at Georgetown Law Center. This student started law school Fall term, so she can take an extra semester in law school and still graduate in Spring term and sit for the bar exam in May, without delaying her bar exam by a year.

We also last year had a JD student law year who attended the LL.M. program at UCLA. The student's legal education and time to full-time employment will be extended by one year, but if all works out he will begin his legal career in Japan with both a KLS JD and he a UCLA LL.M, and he will be admitted to both the Japan and New York bars. (In fact, he has received the UCLA LL.M. and passed the New York State bar exam, so is well on the way to implementing these plans.)

4.1.2 Shorter Term Options

Because of the reluctance of students in Japan to delay graduation and bar exam dates as a result of exchanges, we also offer some other options so that Japanese JD students can get exchange and other legal education experiences outside Japan. A few recent examples follow.

4.1.2.1 University of Washington Summer Institute in Transnational Law

This program, held at the beginning of September every year, offers a two-and-a-half week introduction to American law. Most of the participants in the program are lawyers from around the globe who are about to start the University of Washington LL.M. programs.

Typically, we will send four to six KLS students or recent graduates to participate, as part of our cooperation with the University of Washington School of Law. Many years, a KLS faculty member has taught some of the lectures as well.

GLOBALIZING JAPANESE LEGAL EDUCATION AT KEIO UNIVERSITY LAW SCHOOL ("KLS")

The timing of this program works well not only for current KLS JD students, but for students who obtain their JD in March, take the bar exam in May, complete a short summer internship to line up employment, and then have a gap until they will start the Supreme Court Legal Research and Training Institute 12 month practical training program in December. Again, students who did not have an opportunity to pursue international programs before sitting for the bar exam can do so during this "gap period", with some support from KLS.

4.1.2.2 Melbourne University Law School "Summer School"

This year KLS participated in what had been a longstanding program between the Law Schools of Chuo University and Melbourne University. The program was designed as a class for which a small group of KLS students obtained course credit, with participation and supervision of KLS faculty, but the focus was on Australian law and the Australian legal system, with guest lectures by many Melbourne Law School faculty and visits to courts and law firms in Melbourne.

The program was held in February, in the break between KLS Fall and Spring terms and during Melbourne's southern hemisphere summer vacation.

4.1.2.3 PAGLEP Exchanges

In March 2017 and again in September 2017, KLS faculty led a group of KLS students to visit law schools in Vietnam, Cambodia and Thailand, as part of the PAGLEP exchange program. These programs offer an intensive opportunity for KLS Japanese JD (and, in the future, KLS LL.M.) students, to learn about the legal systems in Southeast Asia, to understand the role of law in economic development, and to form friendships that can become future professional collaborations.

4.1.2.4 International Internships

KLS also offers a limited number of internships at international and foreign institutions, generally between Fall and Spring term. In recent years, students

– 113 –

have completed internships at international organizations involved with cooperation related to outer space and global communication networks. We also now have secured potential opportunities for our LL.M. students to intern with the Singapore courts, in particular the Singapore International Commercial Court.

4.2 LL.M. Exchange Outbound

LL.M. students appear more willing to go on outbound exchanges, and we hope to send our first next Spring.

Especially for Japanese students, we want to encourage a semester exchange as a way to achieve the goals of the LL.M. program. And some non-Japanese LL.M. students also want to spend part of their LL.M. period at another elite university to achieve their academic or career goals. The Keio LL.M. allows them to spend a semester at a much more expensive institution while paying relatively less expensive Keio tuition.

Our LL.M. outbound exchange efforts are still in the early stage, but we have discovered a few things.

- The academic calendar is a problem some places, as the students would need to leave KLS before the end of Fall term, or cannot arrive in time for the beginning of the relevant term.

- Availability of courses, or even basic information, in English is a problem some of the universities with which KLS has exchange agreements. Still, even in non-English speaking countries a significant number of law schools do have an English language curriculum sufficient to permit an exchange without local language fluency.

- For many Japanese students, the TOEFL score requirement at elite US and other law schools can be an issue. We hope that even if at the time of entrance into the KLS program a Japanese student's TOEFL score is not quite high enough to support admission to an elite U.S. law school's LL.M. program, that by studying at KLS for a semester, the student will improve his or her English capability and be more than able to keep up with classwork and participate fully on an exchange program during the second semester of a KLS LL.M.

These are all cautionary points, but we still find that exchange should be possible for our LL.M. students in many cases and for many universities.

4.3 Double Degree LL.M. Program

Our first LL.M. double degree agreement was signed in March, 2017 with the University of Washington School of Law ("UW"). We have had inquiries from some other law schools in Europe and Asia about additional programs and are in discussions on one, though we need to keep the number very limited until we can validate the concept and create a good track record with real examples of students who complete the KLS/UW program and find it beneficial.

Typically, a Keio originating student would spend Spring term at KLS, then Fall and Winter quarters at UW, then return to KLS, and obtain an LL.M. from both institutions, faster and for lower tuition than if both degrees were obtained separately.

We also may consider a Keio LL.M. / foreign J.D. double degree program in the future. This structure might effectively convert some future in-bound exchange students into double degree students, with the result that they would need to complete more rigorous program requirements at KLS. It also would likely increase our tuition income somewhat, as we would not waive tuition for students in a KLS degree program, in constrast to those on bilateral exchanges.

Double degree programs require detailed planning, and we do not yet have a track record with actual implementation. With regard to the KLS/UW arrangement:

- ○ KLS has a single LL.M. in Global Legal Practice.
- ○ UW offers LL.M.'s in 7 areas: Intellectual Property, Tax, Asian Law, Development, Business, Health Law, and a General LL.M.

The double degree arrangement allows a KLS student to get the benefits of the UW specialized programs. Meanwhile, the double degree arrangement allows a UW LL.M. student with a strong interest in Japan to study in Japan and obtain both degrees.

4.3.1 Double Degree and US Bar Admission Requirements.

We did not design the double degree program as a way for KLS LL.M. students to satisfy U.S. bar admission educational prerequisites. Those requirements change from time-to-time, and for some years the New York bar has required those students seeking admission on the basis of their foreign legal education to spend a full academic year in a LL.M. program in classrooms physically located in the United States. Even an American Bar Association ("ABA") accredited law school program located outside of the United States is not sufficient. This means that a semester studying at KLS does not contribute to meeting New York bar admission requirements.

While bar admission requirements require a detailed analysis of individual qualifications, we typically see that for Japanese students who meet the necessary requirements other than the U.S. education component:

○ Fall and Winter quarters at UW is not sufficient to meet requirements for the New York bar. A student would need to spend Spring quarter at UW also.

○ Spring term at Keio, then Fall and Winter quarters at UW, plus one Spring quarter course at UW, ought to be sufficient to qualify to sit for the Washington State Bar, provided that the student meets the other requirements (which, in most cases, would require a Japanese JD or Japan bar membership).

○ To sit for the California Bar, there are no specific LL.M. requirements for lawyers already admitted overseas, but the exam is very hard with the highest score requirements of any U.S. state bar. While there is been some discussion of "lowering the bar" in California by reducing the score requirement, this year a proposal to do so was rejected.

5. Next Steps for KLS Globalization

5.1 Strengthen LL.M. Program and Build a Track Record

We are very happy with the roll-out of our LL.M. program this year. That said, we cannot coast but must take a number of steps to ensure its future success. Especially, we need to build a track record of satisfied, successful students and alumni if we want to recruit thirty excellent students each year easily within Japan and internationally.

We continue to modify and build upon our curriculum, adding additional faculty and offerings in several core areas. A few items to highlight:

- ○ Specialty certificates. We plan to offer Dean's Certificates in a number of specialty areas from 2018 and, if the system works well, to expand it later. The availability of certificates will encourage students to specialize and focus their students. A student can explain the LL.M. to a future employer if she can point to an LL.M. in Global Legal Practice with a Certificate in Business Law or a Certificate in International Dispute Resolution, for example. This is consistent with global trends in post-graduate legal education.

- ○ Japanese language curriculum. In the first year of our program, we have not allowed LL.M. students to access the KLS curriculum taught in Japanese language. We are looking at ways to do this on a limited basis, so that students from outside Japan who have a strong focus on Japanese studies and have already achieved Japanese language fluency can take at least a few of their courses in Japanese, with the J.D. students.

- ○ Even more practical training and distance learning. We are planning to bring in instructors from various places outside of Tokyo who can offer further practice experience and classes that give even more practical training than we do now. Further, we remain eager to try some joint distance-learning classes, including with our PAGLEP partner institutions. We want to give our students a realistic expectation for their future work, and a cross-border negotiation conducted mostly on a "virtual" basis, is a commonplace occurrence outside of the university, and so must become common within the university as well.

5.2 Networks?

In 2015 we were approached about possibly joining with a network of schools, mostly outside of Asia, for exchange programs and an annual jointly held seminar/class. In the end, we decided that the network would create too many conflicts with our existing—already underutilized—outbound exchange partners. That said, if we could find a similar network that did not raise so many conflicts and that closer matched our existing relationships, it would be a very efficient way to conduct exchanges and make progress on globalization of our students' experiences. In this manner, if the PAGLEP network affiliation can be used for programs that we would otherwise need to hold on a purely bi-lateral basis, it can be very efficient.

Similarly, given that many other Japanese law schools do not have the "critical mass" to sponsor global programs such as ours, and that we have more programs available than our students can take advantage of, we think there may be some future benefit if we open some international programs to other Japanese law school participation or offer new programs on a cooperative basis together with other Japanese law schools.

6. Conclusion

KLS has many different efforts underway to globalize the legal education it offers students, and exchange and double degree arrangements are an important component of these efforts.

COMMENTS

JAPANESE LAW TAUGHT IN ENGLISH

Susumu Masuda*
(Keio University Law School)

1. My Presentation Topic

I am a professor at Keio Law School, teaching Private International Law, International Dispute Resolution, and International Finance and Securities Regulations. I have been teaching about half of my courses in English to foreign and Japanese students who wish to study those subjects in English.

My role today is to present a concrete teaching methodology that I used in my English courses at the Keio LL.M. Program in the spring semester, and to hear the panelists' comments, discussions, and critiques.

2. "Cross-Border Litigation" Course

In the 2017 Spring Semester, I taught a course titled, "Cross-Border Litigation," which was comprised of 15 sessions, with each session lasting 90 minutes. The course had 15 enrollees who were very diverse. Fortunately, they included

---

* Professor, Keio University Law School

one African student, two from EU countries, one from the USA, three from Southeast Asian countries, three from China, and five Japanese students. Unfortunately, no students with a background in Islamic-law enrolled.

More than half of the students were licensed lawyers in their home jurisdictions. Among them, there were three native English speakers, which was fewer than I had expected. There were 12 students from civil law jurisdictions and only three from common law jurisdictions. The content of the course is essentially the same as the content normally included in the Private International Law of Japan course, which comprises of Japanese laws concerning international civil procedure, conflict of laws, and enforcement of foreign judgments in Japan.

3. My Teaching Methods

The teaching methods that I used in this course included a lecture and seminar style. In the first part of the class, which normally was 30 to 45 minutes, I lectured on the general explanations of Japanese laws relevant to the day's topics. In the second part, which was normally 45 to 60 minutes, I used a seminar style, which included students' presentations of Japanese court cases, normally two cases per class. Then, we analyzed them and critiqued the judgment under the Japanese law, the students' respective country's laws, and the global perspective.

In leading the analysis, I intentionally used the Socratic Method, which is a US law school-type teaching method with an emphasis on debate and dialog. To enable students to not only stop sleeping in the class but also participate actively in the class and improve their ability to think about and present the law by themselves, I assigned topics and cases to be discussed in each class, and the students were required to prepare for the class in advance. Even though it sounds good, this method was very difficult for me to use.

4. Difficulty (1) – Different Backgrounds

One of the difficulties that I experienced using this teaching method was managing the different backgrounds of the students. First, the structure of laws and legal concepts differed greatly between the civil law system and the common law system. Additionally, the level of globalization in their home countries varied, which was very relevant to the subject of cross-border litigation.

For example, civil law jurisdictions only have only one source of law, which is legislative law. Thus, as Japan is a civil law country, I always introduced Japanese law by repeatedly citing a provision in Code or Act and then explaining why that provision was enacted and how to interpret the wording to apply it to the case in front of us. The students from civil law jurisdictions easily understood my explanations and accepted this method very well because their ways of thinking were very similar.

However, the students from the common law countries always had difficulty and probably felt uneasy about these explanations because they normally perceived that laws were not predetermined in legislations, but were found in court cases. This was the approach of law that was taught in their law schools. Because the common law is not written in a legislative form, their natural approach to thinking about law was through the facts of cases and the analysis of court opinions before referring directly to legislation.

However, this fundamental difference was the major reason that I adopted the lecture and seminar-style teaching in my English classes.

5. Difficulty (2) – English Materials for Japanese Laws

In addition, finding adequate reading materials in English was also challenging. This difficulty seemed to be exasperated by the subject. Cross-border litigation is not a fundamental subject like constitutional law, civil law, and commercial law in Japan. Although it is one of the selected subjects in the Japanese national law examination, it is still not regarded as a major one.

Therefore, it is very hard to find reading materials on this subject in English. Depending on the topic or occasion, I used US or UK legal texts and materials, such as the Nutshell series, which was very handy and compact.

Another efficient method was the use of comparative legal analysis. If students had already studied the same subject in their home country, it was very effective because the student already knew the basic role and concepts of the subject. So, by referring to or citing the legal concept in their home jurisdictions, they generally understood the meanings and functions that the concept had in the subject being discussed.

6. Difficulty (3) – Language

Finally, the language barrier was challenging to overcome. Everybody mentioned this in the morning sessions of the seminar. While technically language was an obstacle, practically it was more an issue of preparation. When students were duly instructed to prepare in advance the reading materials and case presentation, they were very well prepared and completed them successfully in the classes. In that sense, language barriers were minimized because we could use legal terminologies as professionals, and we could easily understand each other.

7. Conclusion

At Keio Law School, in both the JD and the LL.M. programs, at the end of the semester, the students evaluate and grade professors and their teaching methods through questionnaires, and professors are put on notice of the results of the questionnaires. This creates pressure for the professors, but overall, my course was well received by both foreign and Japanese students. Almost all of the students had perfect attendance and actively participated in the class. This is evidence of the positive outcome of the class, in addition to the responses from the questionnaires, which were much better than I had expected.

Finally, I will briefly touch on merits of teaching Japanese laws in English. Of course, this provides language training for lawyers at the professional level. For Japanese students, this provides practice translating or presenting Japanese laws into English, which was a very useful challenge. For foreigners, familiarizing themselves with Japanese legal concepts and terminologies is also valuable so that when they return to their home countries they are able to explain or use Japanese laws in their practices. It was also an excellent opportunity for all of us to exchange legal knowledge from different jurisdictions around the world in the common language of English, and to promote friendship among us.

LOGISTICS FOR
THE IMPLEMENTATION OF
INTERNATIONAL EXCHANGE
PROGRAMS

Hitomi Fukasawa*

(Keio University Law School)

1. Introduction

To promote international exchange programs, we need to overcome several challenges. Table 1 illustrates the processes required to apply for the study of law abroad. According to this table, there are four steps. Step 1 is the conclusion of a MOU or MOA with foreign universities to develop the international programs. Step 2 is the selection of students. Through these two steps, we can make fundamental progress in accepting international students. However, international exchange programs would not be successful through their formation alone. We also need to improve the study environment, both academically and logistically. In my essay, I briefly explain the current issues, including accommodation, financial expenses, and language, and how Keio University Law School (KLS) supports international exchange students logistically. Additionally, I provide suggestions for possible solutions to these challenges.

My observation is based on my working experience at Keio Institute for Global Law and Development (KEIGLAD). I do not rely on any statistical data;

---

* Researcher of Law at Keio Institute for Global Law and Development (KEIGLAD).

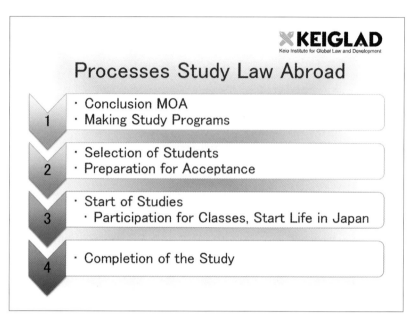

Table 1

This Chart is showing the process study law abroad.
Generally, we can divide 4 steps.
Step 1 is making a condition for exchange program. For example, universities conclude MOA and make study programs.
Step 2 is selection of students and preparation for acceptance.
Step 3 is Start of studies. "Start of Studies" has two aspect: 1 is participation for classes the other start life in Japan.
And step 4 is Completion for study.

however, I believe that this essay is a useful tool for the promotion of international exchange programs.

2. Start Living in Japan

2.1 Accommodation

Safe and reasonably priced accommodations are essential for successful study abroad programs. In Japan, international students have two options, rental

LOGISTICS FOR THE IMPLEMENTATION OF INTERNATIONAL EXCHANGE PROGRAMS

apartment and dormitories.

2.1.1 Apartments

Finding an apartment is quite challenging for international students, not only because of the monthly rent fee but also because of the unfriendly and complicated lease system for foreigners.

Monthly rent fees differ based on the spaces, location, and other facilities. The average price of apartments for students range from 65,000 yen (650 USD) to 80,000 yen (about 800 USD). However, students have to prepare more than 200,000 yen (about 2,000 USD) before they can move to the apartment because, according to Japanese lease custom, a lessee must pay two or three months of rent fees as a security deposit.

Moreover, lessors demand that a lessee provide a guarantor when they conclude a contract. Keio University International Department can serve as a guarantor for international students. Usually, one guarantor is enough, although some lessors demand that foreigners conclude a security contract with a rental guarantee company.

Additionally, apartment owners may have a conservative attitude towards foreigners. Some of them reject foreign lessees, especially ones who cannot communicate in Japanese. These customs and cultures make difficult for international students to find apartments in Japan.

The KLS LL.M. course does not require Japanese language proficiency. The School has tried to be open for international students; however, Japanese society is still in the process of accepting globalization.

Even if the Japanese lease system is not friendly, international students have another option: dormitories.

2.1.2 Dormitories

In Japan, there are two types of dormitories: university dormitories and private dormitories. In this section, my explanation of university dormitories is based on Keio University.

Advantages of dormitories are they do not require students proficient in Japanese.

Both university and private dormitory facilities are almost same, having dorm managers, individual rooms, common spaces, and meal services. However, they are different in price and the level of student support provided.

Private dormitories are less expensive than apartments; however, they are expensive when compared with university dormitories. Moreover, university dormitories have "Residential Assistant" (RA) students that provide support for international students' daily lives. University dormitories provide good services for international students.

In conclusion, university dormitories are the best option for international students.

2.1.3 Accommodation Support by KLS

KLS applies for dormitories for international students. However, all students cannot stay in university dormitories because of the limited number of rooms. In the Fall Semester 2017, KLS accepted four students from our PAGLEP partner universities, two are official students in the LL.M. course and the others are exchange students. KLS could only find Keio dormitories for two exchange students. However, the other two students have to live in private dormitories. We need to consider possible solution for future programs.

2.1.4 Possible Solution

The accommodation problem cannot be solved at the law school level. This issue should be addressed at a university level.

As of April 2017, Keio University has eight dormitories and two new dormitories are under construction. In 2018, Keio University will have ten dormitories and will be able to accept one thousand five hundred and twenty four students in total.[1] However, it is believed that ten dormitories are still not enough to accept a

---

[1] Keio University, "Press Release" (April 17, 2017), https://www.keio.ac.jp/ja/press-releases/

significant number of international students.

2.2 Tuition and Cost of Living

2.2.1 Tuition and Cost of Living

The KLS LL.M. course tuition fee is 1,632,240 yen (about 14,360 USD). Because of the cost, it is a difficult for students to decide whether to study in Japan or not.

In addition, students have to pay for living expenses. Japan is known as one of the most expensive countries in the world. Living expenses differ depending on each student's lifestyle. According to the Keio University SFC Global Information and Academic Program, the average monthly living cost, including housing fees, daily meals, and transportation in Kanto area, which includes Tokyo, is about 154,000 yen (about 1,350 USD)[2].

Therefore, it costs approximately, 3,500,000 yen (about 31,255USD) for one year study in Japan. While, the high financial cost is not the only reason that students choose not to study in Japan, it is a significant deterrent. Some students decline their admission even though they pass the entrance exam. Universities should consider providing financial support to encourage foreign students to study in Japan.

2.2.2 Financial Support from KLS

Regarding tuition, in exchange programs with partner universities, students are mutually exempted from paying tuition at the foreign university because they pay tuition to their home universities.

This exemption does not apply to students who study as an official student in the KLS LL.M. course. However, there is an option for students who perform

---

files/2017/4/17/170417-1.pdf, last accessed October 30, 2017, (available only Japanese).

[2] Keio University SFC Global Information and Academic "7. Living Expense in Japan", 2015, http://ic.sfc.keio.ac.jp/uploads/2015/07/7.-Living-expenses-in-Japan.pdf, last accessed October 30, 2017.

well on the entrance examination to be exempted from the payment of tuition.

KLS can also provide support for monthly living costs to some extent. We support round trip airfare and monthly rent fees for students who come from PAGLEP partner universities. This support does not cover other daily expenses, such as meals, transportation, and other living expenses. However, students who are qualified can apply for scholarships from the Japan Student Service Organization (JASSO). The scholarship is about 70,000 yen (around 700 USD).

2.2.3 Possible Solutions and Challenges

I conclude that KLS provides enough financial support to international students from our PAGLEP partner universities. However, this program still has issues.

(1) Limitation of Budget

The biggest issue is that our budget is limited. The PAGLEP program gets financial support from the Ministry of Education in Japan. This financial support will reduce year by year. It is unclear whether KLS can support students at the same level of quality every year. Moreover, this financial support will expire in 2020.

(2) Expensive Tuition and Limited Availability of Scholarships

Another issue is related to tuition and scholarships. As I mentioned in section 2.2.2, tuition fees are mutually exempted among partner universities for exchange programs. However, students can not enjoy this benefit without the conclusion of a MOA between KLS and their home university. Moreover, this rule does not apply to KLS LL.M. course official students. While KLS can provide these official students with a scholarship, it is only available for a few students. JASSO also has a limited amount of available scholarship funds.

(3) Possible Solution for Future Programs

To address the international exchange programs' dependence on the budget from the Ministry of Education and KLS, we should seriously consider independent funding from companies, organizations, and other institutions.

3. Other Obstacles Abroad—The Language Barrier

In Chapter 1 and Chapter 2, I explained logistical issues related to accommodations and finances. In Chapter 3, I consider the challenge of overcoming language barriers for the study law abroad.

3.1 Using Japanese in Daily Life

The KLS LL.M. course's unique policy is that all classes are provided in English. This policy overcame any language barrier in the study of law in Japan because Japanese was essential for study in the past. However, in life outside of campus, Japanese is required. Most of guidance and information boards are written in English. The number of Japanese people who speak English is also increasing. However, sometimes students have to use Japanese, for example, when they go to a city office to register for their residence; when they open bank account; or when they go to a hospital. Sometimes they have to write in Japanese. People must write their application forms in Japanese to open bank account. Even though bank staff are often able to communicate in English, students need some support in Japanese.

3.2 Possible Solution

PAGLEP has started a tutoring system to support international students. The tutors are Japanese and international students that have studied in Japan for more than one semester. In 2017, seven students, including six Japanese students registered as tutors. They support the international students, not only in their study but also their daily lives. When international students need help in Japanese, the tutors support them. Sometimes they accompany the international students to complete tasks that require Japanese proficiency. In September of 2017, five tutors supported international students to enter dorms and open bank accounts. This tutoring system is successful and helps to build friendships between Japanese and international students.

4. Conclusion

In this essay, I briefly explained the logistical challenges to studying abroad and implementing the PAGLEP program. Some of our practices have succeeded, but others still face challenges. In particular, issues related to accommodation and securing funding are urgent. We need to consider receiving contributions from new institutions and other novel measures to secure funding independently.

PANEL DISCUSSION

PANEL DISCUSSION

How Can We Promote
International Exchange Programs
for the Study of Law among Universities
in the Asian Region?

Participants

Myanmar

Professor Khin Chit Chit

Professor Khin Phone Myint Kyu

Thailand

Professor Viravat Chantachote

Professor Junavit Chalidabhongse

Laos

Assoc. Professor Viengvilay Thiengchanhxay

Ms. Sonenaly Nanthavong

Cambodia

Professor Kong Phallack

Professor Phin Sovath

Vietnam

Assoc. Professor Vu Thi Lan Anh

Assoc. Professor Nguyen Van Quang

Professor Nguyen Ngoc Dien

Mr. Le Van Hinh

Japan

Professor David Litt

Professor Susumu Masuda,

Ms. Hitomi Fukasawa

Moderator

Professor Hiroshi Matsuo

Hiroshi Matsuo:

Let me start our discussion on the central theme of this meeting about how we can promote international exchange programs for the study of law among universities in the Asian region. It will include three major topics.

First, we need to identify the current problems and obstacles to overcome for the promotion of international exchange study programs between us. We know that there are differences in the academic calendar,

– 137 –

which varies for each university. This variance becomes an obstacle to the arrangement of exchange programs, especially when we begin taking applications and when we accept students. How we can promote short and middle term exchange study programs? How do we set our goals and achieve them? How do we give more students the opportunity to join a program? How do we give credit points and evaluate the students? What is the domestic procedure to arrange exchange programs? We cannot forget the language barrier with which many foreign students are tackling.

Second, we will confirm the current practices to enhance the international exchange programs. For instance, some ASEAN universities have created an arrangement called the ASEAN University Network (AUN) to facilitate inter-university cooperation. They invite teachers and arrange intensive study programs. They also have the ASEAN Credit Transfer System (ACTS). It is a system to reassign credit points. It enables member universities to make collaborative study programs and transfer credits points.

Third, on the basis of the current practices, we will be able to reduce obstacles make things go forward by improving them. For instance, How about making a network like the AUN to promote exchange programs? It will be extended to the promotion of university teachers and officers exchange programs, the arrangement of intensive courses to study the theory and practice of foreign laws, etc. They will create new opportunities for students. We will not forget to discuss about logistic issues for the implementation of exchange programs.

I believe we now share various obstacles that we need to overcome to facilitate international exchange programs both for students and for teachers. Let me start from the difference in the semester terms. Every university has its own rules of calendar. Please look at page 176 and 177 of Comparative Legal Education from Asian Perspective [ed. by KEIGLAD, 2017], which was distributed to all of you this morning. There is a comparative table of the semesters at all the partner universities of the Programs for Asian Global Legal Professions (PAGLEP). You can confirm the be-

– 138 –

PANEL DISCUSSION: How Can We Promote International Exchange Programs for the Study of Law among Universities in the Asian Region?

ginning and the end of each semester and its duration at our partner universities. You will see that the university calendar so varies that it is not easy for us to arrange collaborative programs. This year [in 2017], we have conducted joint programs from March 6 to 20 with the University of Economics and Law in Ho Chi Minh, Vietnam, and Paññāsāstra University in ⌐Phnom Penh, Cambodia. We also had a summer seminar from August 20 to 28 in Tokyo. We held a joint seminar from September 12 to 18 at Thammasat University in Bangkok, Thailand. Since these short-term joint programs can be arranged between a week and 10 days fairly flexibly in spite of the semester gaps, they should be maintained and improved next year. They will include (a) special lectures by teachers from both sides of participant universities, (b) presentations and discussions by students from both sides on the common topic presented by the teacher(s) and prepared by the students in advance. (c) The joint programs also incorporate class observation of some normal lectures. There are many interesting courses and seminars worth visiting at each

university. In addition, (d) excursions will help students learn about the history and the cultures of each country and they are also encouraged. The short-term joint programs may also be held in Vientiane, Yangon and Hanoi. On the other hand, the gap of term problem becomes more serious problem when we arrange the longer joint programs which last 3 months, 6 months or longer. If you have any comments or queries on possible obstacles, or other remarks you would like to make, please feel free to raise your hands. Yes, Professor Junavit, please.

Junavit Chalidabhongse:

Thank you very much Professor Matsuo and thank you all for the wonderful presentation today. The issue that Professor Matsuo has raised is quite interesting because we actually have different schedules at our universities. Although I find the idea quite interesting, Thammasat does not offer many short-term modules. The question to ask, I feel, is what the desired objective of such short-term programs would be and what our students would achieve from them. I

– 139 –

Discussants (from left) : Professor Nguyen Ngoc Dien; Professor Phin Sovath.

do not think it would be possible for students to imbibe the knowledge of a full 3 or 4 month course in one week or even one month. From the point of view of the university, a credit for such a short module may not be possible. However, the department or the Faculty of Law may find it possible to certify that a student has attended the short exchange session. Students may garner some fundamental information from the short module, which would have to be specifically designed to achieve a focused objective so that students may attain the knowledge the university desires them to realize in the short term. Thank you.

Hiroshi Matsuo:

Thank you very much, Professor Junavit. The short-term program is a sampler of the cooperative programs, and it could be viewed as one of the entrance points to the joint programs. The brief version is easier to arrange and implement, and it benefits students in terms of easy access in participating in international coursework. However, as Professor Junavit indicated, this short version is not enough to help students gain an in-depth understanding of the legal system or for them to conduct comparative research in law. So we require other longer programs to be instituted, to which the short-term programs may be on the entry points. Thank you. I will now call upon Professor Dien.

Nguyen Ngoc Dien:

PANEL DISCUSSION: How Can We Promote International Exchange Programs for the Study of Law among Universities in the Asian Region?

Discussants (from left) : Associate Professor Viengvilay Thiengchanhxay; Dr.Junavit Chalidabhongse and Dr.Viravat Chantachote.

To my opinion, credit transfers are problematic and we should be careful about offering them. In my experience, only one or two students go abroad to a foreign university in the present framework of exchange. If they only stay 1 or 2 weeks, a credit transfer would be practically impossible because we cannot organize special courses to serve only a couple of learners from another country. In order for a foreign student to earn a credit, the only solution would be to mix, to immerse, and to totally integrate the foreign students with a class of domestic students in a manner that they have to work closely with their peers from the host university.

With only a few students participating in the current exchange format and the mandate that we are to conduct the courses in the English language, it is even more necessary for foreign learners to stay for at least a full semester. Regular English lectures are given weekly at our university and imparting any useful learning in a week or two is unfeasible. In such a short time, we could, perhaps only hold collaborative or group study workshops for a couple of foreign students. On the other hand, it would be possible to easily organize special classes at Thammasat for a larger group comprising between 10 and 20 foreign students who could, in a week

Discussants (from left) : Professor Susumu Masuda; Professor Hiroshi Matsuo and Ms. Hitomi Fukasawa.

or two, go through an intensive program of a very focused curriculum in a particular area of law.

This eventuality depends upon our interaction with our partner institutions. At this juncture, I would like to inform my colleague from Thammasat University about the ACTS Program. ACTS is a system of credit transfers among ASEAN universities, and within this program we welcome students coming from universities located in the ASEAN region, for example, from Thammasat. In fact, we are soon about to welcome a student from Chiang Mai University, Thailand.

We have only two requirements from this student: first, she has to speak either English or Vietnamese; second, she has to accept the condition of staying with us for at least one semester. The reason for this stipulation is that if she comes to our university only for a couple of weeks, she has to take classes with French-speaking students and in any case, she would only be able to focus on one or two topics of study before she had to return to her home university.

It is fortunate that this particular student has decided to remain with us for the full semester. It is definitely better for her because with this length of stay, she will have enough time to follow different courses. The experience would be interesting to her and she would have the opportunity to communicate with the Vietnamese

PANEL DISCUSSION: How Can We Promote International Exchange Programs for the Study of Law among Universities in the Asian Region?

students, not only on the subject of law but on all matters related to cultural and social life.

Hiroshi Matsuo:

Thank you very much, Processor Dien. Our summer seminar held this August was only a 9-day event but every day, our students took part in two 90-minute classes. If we calculate the teaching hours of a semester's coursework as 15 weeks of active instruction with one 90 minute class per week, the number of hours attended by exchange students in those 9 days becomes comparable. I can say that there may be some subjects of law for which a full semester's learning can be actually imparted into those intensive instructions and discussions. As Professor Junavit asked the purpose of the short term programs, they are focused on particular and independent topic of common interest and attractive for participants from abroad. Professor Dien has raised the problem of credit transfers, and this is already standardized in the ACTS system for ASEAN countries with regard to workload and learning outcomes.

It is interesting for us to com-

municate our ideas and opinions on the minimum standards for offering credits and we should come to a consensus on this issue. If there are any ideas or comments on this topic, please make your proposals at this time.

Nguyen Ngoc Dien:

In order to implement ACTS, we have to accomplish a great deal of groundwork. First, we have to share and compare our curricula and come to a mutual understanding with regard to the inclusion of certain topics in every syllabus imparted by the partner universities. For example, for an economic curriculum, we have macroeconomics as a topic at a general level. An identical subject matter exists in the curriculum of our partner Thammasat University. With agreement and acknowledgment, both institutions could allot the same number of credits for this particular course.

Hence, the students would have the flexible option of either staying at the home university for the entire duration of such a course or following a part of the coursework at a partner university in another ASEAN country as a component of the exchange program. In such a scenario, if the student decides to complete the coursework at a foreign university that is a partner to the program, the home university would validate the credits without any problem. This system would allow a student to easily move within the network of the partner universities to follow courses in English and avail of exchange opportunities over the entire period of study.

Hiroshi Matsuo:

The idea that the students should also integrate to other learners in the existing programs in each partner university is very appealing and could be viable in the future. However, the differences in term schedules among countries might be still an impediment in the implementation of such ideas, especially for those who are outside of the ACTS framework. So that some special programs of short-term unit is just one idea, and we need various kinds of programs to successfully execute international students and to be faculty exchange initiative. Perhaps some intensive courses to be held over the holidays between the terms. Are there any other ideas or comments?

Junavit Chalidabhongse:

Yes, I would like to also discuss my views about the credit transfer system. I also agree with Professor Dien about the issue of the transfer credit system. I think we should conduct an international program. If we do not, it would be really difficult to take a course at another university because even if the students travel to study for the entire semester, they would require a course to be taught in English.

In order to transfer credits, the curriculum must be quite balanced at all partner universities. I do not think it can be done at the moment, from my experience. We now also have the AUN Program but I can find that only 30 universities that are members of the ASEAN in the AUN.

I am also interested in the issue that was raised by the delegation from Hanoi Law University regarding the establishment of the ASEAN University Legal Network. I think it is very interesting idea which is worth exploring.

PANEL DISCUSSION: How Can We Promote International Exchange Programs for the Study of Law among Universities in the Asian Region?

Discussants (from left) : Associate Professor Nguyen Van Quang; Associate Professor Vu Thi Lan Anh and Mr. Le Van Hinh.

Hiroshi Matsuo:

Professor Quang, please.

Nguyen Van Quang:

I have some comments on the same question that Professor Matsuo raised. First of all, we can also quite easily include in some short-term processes in the International Institute Exchange Program. So we can include 1 week or 10 days or even a month in the program quite easily. The issue of whether or not to recognize the credits depends very much on the bilateral agreement between the two law schools.

We are currently conducting an International Exchange Program with Waikato University in New Zealand. That course takes about 4 weeks and Waikato recognized all credits that their students take at my university and we discussed the potential issues in a very detailed manner. Matters such as the organization of the cost structure, the coursework, and the method of assessment were all debated in advance. As an example, after 4 weeks, students would be required to write an original essay of about 1000 words in English along with one oral presentation. Professors from both Waikato and Hanoi Law University would attend the session and then co-grade the student's presentation. After the presentation, the student's assignment would be marked.

If the student is successful, Waikato would recognize the credits that their students accumulated during the coursework they attended in Hanoi. Thus, it depends totally on the bilateral agreement between the home and the partner law school.

As far as Keio University is concerned, we can easily include the 1-week special course in our curriculum for exchange students and as long as we have at least a group of 7 or 10 students coming from Keio, we can easily organize the Student Program. Whether or not you will recognize the credits, depends entirely on you. We would be very happy to follow the instructions of your law school. That is the first point I would like to mention here.

Second, as I mentioned in my presentation about the Asian Law School network, I like the idea very much because if we create a very good network, we can discuss any difficulties we face during the implementation of the International Exchange Program. For example, if we have that network, we could draw all the professors of the law school in the network to discuss problems and to design some common courses taught in English such as an introduction to the legal system of a particular country.

If our students come to Thammasat to study a semester, there should be a course called the Introduction to Thai Legal System or something similar. If we receive some students from Thammasat University to my institution, the curriculum would include an introduction to the Vietnamese legal system. That is one course we can easily agree upon among the law schools.

We can design some international law related courses and these courses can be taught at any law school within the network. Examples of such curricula could be international trade law, commercial law or similar topics. These are some of the benefits of building a network.

As an added advantage, we could understand very clearly the structure of degree programs of each law school within the network. Thus, we could easily work on the bilateral agreement with each other and once we had an agreement between two law schools, we could easily apply the international exchange programs among the two law schools. That is the idea.

PANEL DISCUSSION: How Can We Promote International Exchange Programs for the Study of Law among Universities in the Asian Region?

Beyond that, the network would also be beneficial for the broad aspects of the ASEAN integration objectives. Once we build that network, we could promote legal education in the region in the near future. Thus, students who graduate from Thammasat could perhaps practice law in Vietnam in Hanoi or law students who graduate from Hanoi Law University could come to work in the Philippines or Indonesia.

Hiroshi Matsuo:

Thank you for the very concrete and the viable proposals to extend and create the international exchange programs. Professor Phallack will speak next.

Kong Phallack:

Yeah, thank you for giving me the opportunity to share my views. Before I talk, I want to first clarify the theme of the discussion. We are talking today about a method through which we can accept international students. This implies that each university here can host Keio students or students from other partner universities. We have to first discuss whether we would like to do so. In our past experience, PUC has hosted Keio students and we created a special spring course and seminar for this purpose.

This syllabus was not part of the existing curriculum but we had the flexibility of selecting what we wanted to impart. I want to hear from the group and discuss the possibilities of creating inter-university courses such as, for instance a short course on the Cambodian law of income tax.

We have that course in our Master Program and there are multiple topics in the syllabus ranging from an introduction to the legal system, the consumer law and also economic and labor law. Civil procedure and civil court are also taught among the more than like 20 legal topics. This course, thus, encompasses a general understanding of Cambodian law as a whole. In this course, we can host any student from the ASEAN countries if they are interested in Cambodian law. We can also accommodate Japanese students if they want to understand Cambodian law and also help the Japanese companies to operate their businesses in the Kingdom of Cambodia.

– 147 –

Discussants (from left) : Professor Kong Phallack; Associated professor Viengvilay Thiengchanhxay and Ms. Sonenaly Nanthavong.

This is the existing course. To inform everyone, we have a course of 48 hours and three credits, so one credit is 16 hours. We could have an internal arrangement of approximately 30-hour lectures, 10-hours of practical work and 8-hours of assessment for a mid-term grade and also for our foreign students. So, professors would have the flexibility of execution when they are assigned to teach any particular course.

I am trying to reflect on how we could make this cooperation under the project fruitful and beneficial for everyone. Perhaps we could build one single course that students from all the partner universities could take and the credit from that course would be recognized by each university. We could designate an existing course for this purpose or create a new course. However, the credits would depend on the hours of the course at the university. I think even the hours of instruction are not so different among our universities.

At our university, we have the flexibility of creating an elective course and including the law curriculum within it, but we have a process of approving the course at the faculty level and then gaining acceptance from the University Academic Program Office in order to receive a code, because each course have the course code and the course code is provided by the university, such as Law 501 or Law 505.

I just wanted to air this idea and

PANEL DISCUSSION: How Can We Promote International Exchange Programs for the Study of Law among Universities in the Asian Region?

perhaps we would need to come up with a clear roadmap of discussions between each university and Keio, or we could discuss a common program for the students from Laos, and we could take turns to teach that course at each university and also have professors from different universities to teach it.

In my time at my university, we have created a course called human rights in Southeast Asia that was just approved last month for this term and we have invited a professor from Mahidol to teaching today and tomorrow in Cambodia. Two weeks ago, we had a professor from the National University Vietnam, Hanoi Law School for lectures, and next month we will welcome a professor from the Philippines to teach that course. We thus have four professors, including the home professors, teaching that course because it is a comprehensive issue in the ASEAN mechanism.

This is just one of the examples. A cooperation started between a professor at Vietnam National University and myself. We have no funding. Both our universities have no funding but we thought of this interest and

we looked for funding to implement the program. Vietnam National University Law School also started that course, and now the same course is taught in both Cambodia and in Vietnam. I also teach in Vietnam for 1 week for that course.

When we considered the design of that course, we realized that professors are willing to travel but for a short time. Nevertheless, after the visiting professors leave, the course needs to continue for the home university to complete the credit requirement. We have not begun the exchange of the students yet because it is very expensive. However, this is another kind of cooperation.

The exchange of instructors also improves our teaching skills. I have my students record what they learned from the Vietnamese professors, from the Thai professor, or the Philippine professor. In analyzing the teaching methodology of different professors, we can try to improve our own abilities as well.

Hiroshi Matsuo:

Thank you very much, Professor Phallack. The newly created international cooperation program on human rights in Southeast Asia seems to be informative. How long each of the four professors stayed in Phnom Penh to teach this course on human rights of each country?

Kong Phallack:

Normally, the students have to take that course only 1 day a week but when we fly in professors it is expensive. Thus, we have intensive teaching and when the visiting professor comes to the university, we give the availability by the flexibility of time to the professor and also the amount of money that we can budget. A professor may choose to take three requests, where one request is 3 hours, amounting to a total of 12 hours of instruction. We then request the professor to provide one public seminar, so that everyone, not only the students in the class, can attend.

Professors stay at our university only three nights but the students agree to work harder to gain from the experience of gaining instruction from foreign professors. So when the Vietnamese professors visit, our students study and work full-time on Saturday morning, afternoon and also one Sunday morning because of the schedule of the professor. The professors fly in on a Friday and they stay on Friday night, Saturday night, and Sunday night and then they leave in the morning on Monday.

The students also feel that they can relax because we just follow the topics in the course syllabus. Like this week, the professor from Mahidol University, will just stay in Cambodia for 3 days and return on Monday but she will teach the whole day.

Hiroshi Matsuo:

Okay. So it is very flexible arrangement of the special courses and, if teachers and students both participate in the program, it would become one of the extensions of the international exchange programs. Thank you very much. Are there any other questions on this emerging framework?

Khin Chit Chit:

We always need to get prior permission from the Ministry of Education when foreign professors come to my department to deliver a special lecture, and when students

PANEL DISCUSSION: How Can We Promote International Exchange Programs for the Study of Law among Universities in the Asian Region?

Discussants (from left) : Professor Khin Phone Mynt Kyu and Professor Khin Chit Chit.

want to go abroad for the Students Exchange Program, we always have to take permission from the Ministry of Education. It is very different from Cambodia.

Hiroshi Matsuo:

May I ask how long it takes to get permission to invite a professor or a teacher?

Khin Chit Chit:

We always take permission from the rector and then we get permission from the Higher Department Education and then the Ministry of Education, so that it takes a long time.

[Male Participant/ Nguyen Ngoc Dien/ Virawat Chantachote]:

I would like to add some more information about the ACTS Program because we are actually a member of the ASEAN University Network (AUN). I think we should have a leader for the law university, for example, after the University of Indonesia now is the Secretariat of the AUN and they create a network of the member universities.

On the website, they show all subjects of similarity among the universities. For example, when they show the subjects of economics and law, Chiang Mai University students see the subject and I see the similarity and I apply. And when Chiang Mai University apply and we can see larger application, within which there was a similar course with the University

− 151 −

of Economics and Law and we say, okay, please come and study.

But the problem is with the quality assurance between the universities. When the Chiang Mai University students come to our university in one semester and when they come back to Chiang Mai University, whether the credit earned at UEL will be valuable at Chiang Mai is the big problem. If the credit is not valuable at Chiang Mai University, that student statement becomes invalid. In conclusion, we should have a legal university to create the network.

Hiroshi Matsuo:

Thank you. We have talked about the credit transfer and it is already implemented in some ASEAN universities. So, each university has its own evaluation system to give credit. Sometimes it is a written examination or an original essay, and/or a presentation, and/or an oral examination. Are there any standards of evaluation to make a credit transfer and to mutually recognize the credit? If you have some information about this evaluation standard to exchange credits, could you tell us about it? I guess a

common set of standards of the evaluation is required.

Nguyen Ngoc Dien:

There are two phases for the management of credit transfers in terms of preparation. In the first phase, there must be a comparison of the examination and a comparison of the concerned curricula to define a set of subject matters which could be taught to students to obtain credit transfer. Experts will be invited to constitute a working team to proceed with the comparison and evaluation.

After phase one, we arrive to establish a list of courses which could be taught within the framework of the credit transfer. The second phase is the signing of an agreement between the partner universities. With this agreement, the list as established by the group of experts will be validated and will become a legal document to be used as the very basis of the credit transfer.

Only after completing these two phases, we may proceed because we cannot allow our students to travel without any guarantees after the evaluation of credits. When we receive a

PANEL DISCUSSION: How Can We Promote International Exchange Programs for the Study of Law among Universities in the Asian Region?

student, we must take responsibility for his or her stay in terms of security as well is in terms of academic education.

So the students just spend their time following courses. The evaluation and the recognition of credits to be transferred depend on the authorities of the partner universities.

Hiroshi Matsuo:

Thank you very much, Professor Dien. May I ask for some questions or comments from the audience? I am very grateful to all the participants who are attending this meeting, and some foreign students have also joined us. If you have any comments or questions or requests to reduce the obstacles or to lower the barriers, please feel free to raise your hands. Before speaking, please identify yourself.

Hitomi Fukasawa:

My name is Hitomi Fukasawa, a researcher from Keio Institute for Global Law and Development (KEI-GLAD). I have a question about the Exchange Program in your country. I am arranging an Exchange Program

for Japanese students and if this is successful, we can organize similar Exchange Programs in Thailand, Ho Chi Minh City and Phnom Penh and that program would be a short-term course of between 1 week and 10 days.

At Keio Law School (KLS), we would like to send our students for 6 months or 1 year to study law abroad. However, as you know, at KLS, most students are enrolled in the Judicial Doctor course, and they have to take the bar examination after their graduation from the university. After taking the bar examination, however, they have a gap term of about 3 to 4 months between May and September while they are waiting for the results.

If possible, we would like to send our students to your universities during this period. However, I checked the academic calendar, but every school has already started before May, so that the students cannot attend the beginning of the class in May. I would be interested in whether students are allowed to enroll in the middle of the semester. Is it possible for our students to participate in a course from the middle of the semes-

– 153 –

ter?

Hiroshi Matsuo:

This is a very practical question regarding the implementation of the Exchange Program to send students from Keio University. Professor Viravat will answer.

Viravat Chantachote:

I would like to clarify my understanding of your question. The students would like to go and study and not just for relaxation. They would get the credits but they would enroll at the middle of the term. How can I tell my own students to join us during the middle term and they will get the credit and they can take the exam after term has lapsed for 2 months or something like that?

Nguyen Van Quang:

I can answer your question from the Hanoi Law University perspective. In my university, we offer two kinds of courses. One is a 50 week course, and in that course you must enroll in the first semester. The second tie-up course is what we call the 5-week intensive course. This means

if the 5-week intensive course can begin or start in May, your students can come to study with us but it very much depends on the academic calendar of the law schools in the region. In my university's case, we can offer it, but please make sure that we have to be apprised in advance as we cannot offer the 5-week intensive course every semester.

Hiroshi Matsuo:

Thank you very much. We understand that a special course such as a 5-week course needs to be arranged. Any other comments? Yes, Professor Viravat.

Viravat Chantachote:

It seemed to me that for Hanoi Law University it should be no problem, because we, Hanoi Law University and Thammasat University start the academic year from September and the students can definitely visit. We do not conduct an international program but the students from Japan come and choose to study in English. That is why we have a doubt. Otherwise, we can assign the students to take a seat and study with the stu-

PANEL DISCUSSION: How Can We Promote International Exchange Programs for the Study of Law among Universities in the Asian Region?

dents as much as possible. That is our situation.

Hiroshi Matsuo:

Okay, thank you. Any other views? Yes, Professor Phallack.

Kong Phallack:

Hitomi wanted to know when you want to send the Japanese students. Your students may stay between two semesters at my university. We have our first semester between around April 20 to August 20. If your students can come in May, they would just miss 1-week's lectures, and usually the first week is just an introduction to the course syllabus.

The new term begins on August 28. I think if we can discuss it further, we can find a way to accept your students at PUC. I think for that period it will not be an issue for us. And now we have the internet, they can work online and submit their reports online afterwards. If they fail to submit their reports, they do not get credit.

Hitomi Fukasawa:

Okay, I understand. Thank you, Phallack sensei.

Hiroshi Matsuo:

Thank you, Professor Phallack, for your positive comment. Yes, Professor Dien please.

Nguyen Ngoc Dien:

The university calendars of the partners being quite different, it is very difficult to organize the movement of Japanese students to universities located in ASEAN countries. However, I think another solution is possible, so we can organize special courses during the summer between May and September.

Normally, in May, the semester is all but finished. There is only a revision for examinations, and after the final exams, the domestic students are on vacation. Some of our students do enroll for summer courses, so if it is possible, I think we can deal with the possibility of integrating Japanese students to our framework of summer courses on the condition that these summer courses are interesting to Japanese students.

Another solution could be the organization of special courses just in service of Japanese students. In this case, you must send a reasonable number of students, for example, between 10 and 20 for such a course to be viable.

Hiroshi Matsuo:

Thank you, Professor Dien, for showing us the concrete and viable ideas of special courses. Any other comments? Yes, Professor Khin Chit Chit, please.

Khin Chit Chit:

Yangon University is on vacation in May, and classes begin again from the beginning of June to the third week of September, so we can accept students. But your university and my university would have to sign a MOU or a MOA and if you want to attend these classes, you would have to send a proposal 6 months ahead of the beginning of the course.

Hiroshi Matsuo:

Thank you, Professor Khin Chit Chit. The first semester of Yangon University starts from the beginning of June, so it is the best fit for our students to also complete their first semester in Yangon University. Inter-

estingly among ASEAN universities the university calendars vary. Any other questions or comments? Yes, Professor Ortolani, please.

Andrea Ortolani:

My name is Andrea Ortolani, Keio University, Faculty of Law. I teach undergraduate students. Of course, logistical aspects are very important but when these are resolved, there are the substantive aspects. The two themes that I heard in all your presentations were the language and the comparative facets of law that must be worked out.

I teach comparative law and some of your presentations touched upon the aspects of comparative law. If somebody has comments or remarks on the status of comparative law in your countries, I would be very much interested.

I know that we are also short of time, so I will not ask you to describe the detailed report. However, some comments on the status on the situation of comparative law in your curriculum, in your countries would be highly useful. Thank you.

PANEL DISCUSSION: How Can We Promote International Exchange Programs for the Study of Law among Universities in the Asian Region?

Hiroshi Matsuo:

Thank you very much, Professor Ortolani. It was one of the major topics in the First Meeting of Comparative Legal Education on March 4, 2017. Some participant universities recognized the subject concerning comparative law in the curriculum ... Yeah, Professor, go on.

Nguyen Van Quang:

A quick answer to your question. At my university, we also include the comparative law but as an elective course. We have an institution we call the Institution for Comparative Law, which is just a center but now we have promoted it as an Institute of Comparative Law. In that institute, we offer a comparative law course and we conduct many studies in order to support the teaching and research.

Hiroshi Matsuo:

Thank you very much. Yes, Professor Khin Chit Chit.

Khin Chit Chit:

As for Yangon University, we have one subject for an elective course on comparative public law. We

have especially focused on the main legal systems, common law system, civil law system and then the state practice.

Hiroshi Matsuo:

Thank you very much for your kind answer. Now we are over the scheduled time. I feel that we could exchange frank opinions very positively for the further improvement of our joint programs and to develop our mutual exchange of students and teachers. I found that we need to start careful negotiations for the construction of basic framework of joint programs including credit transfer. I believe we could identify and share the problems before us, the causes of those issues and the direction of the future solutions.

I would like to thank again all the presenters and commentators and also acknowledge all the students and the participants attending this Meeting.

Participants Details

Myanmar

Professor Khin Chit Chit, Department of Law, University of Yangon

Professor Khin Phone Myint Kyu, Department of Law, University of Yangon

Thailand

Professor Viravat Chantachote, Chairman of the Curriculum Review and Development, Faculty of Law, Thammasat University

Professor Junavit Chalidabhongse, Assistant Dean, Faculty of Law, Thammasat University

Laos

Assoc. Professor Viengvilay Thiengchanhxay, Dean, Faculty of Law and Political Science (FLP), National University of Laos (NUOL)

Ms. Sonenaly Nanthavong, Head of International Cooperation Unit, FLP, NUOL

Cambodia

Professor Kong Phallack, Dean, Faculty of Law and Public Affairs, Paññāsāstra University of Cambodia (PUC-FLPA)

Professor Phin Sovath, Assistant Dean in charge of Graduate Law Programs, PUC-FLPA

Vietnam

Assoc. Professor Vu Thi Lan Anh, Vice Rector, Hanoi Law University

Assoc. Professor Nguyen Van Quang, Hanoi Law University

Professor Nguyen Ngoc Dien, Vice Rector, University of Economics and Law (UEL)

Mr. Le Van Hinh, Deputy Head of UEL's International Relation Office, UEL

Japan

Professor David G. Litt, Keio University Law School

Professor Susumu Masuda, Keio University Law School

Ms. Hitomi Fukasawa, Researcher of Keio Institute for Global Law and Development (KEIGLAD), Keio University Law School

Professor Hiroshi Matsuo, Director of KEIGLAD, Keio University Law School

ON-SITE REPORTS

SPECIAL SUMMER PROGRAM ON COMPARATIVE AND INTERNATIONAL BUSINESS LAW SHORT REPORT

Mao Kimpav*

1. Introduction

The Special Summer Program on Comparative and International Business Law was held from August 21 to 29, 2017, at Keio University Law School, Tokyo, Japan. This program provided opportunities to PUC-FLPA students (Cambodia); other students from Laos, Myanmar, and Vietnam; and KLS students to learn about the comparative and international business law and practice in each country. Similarly, a special seminar on Cambodian and Japanese law was hosted by the PUC-FLPA in March 2017, where students from both the KLS and the FLPA had an opportunity to learn about and discuss Cambodian law, Japanese law, and the practice in each country. The aim of the Special Summer Program on Comparative and International Business Law was to bring together students from ASEAN countries (Cambodia, Laos, Myanmar, and Vietnam) and Japan (KLS) to learn about international trade law, international law on sale of goods and its development, the development of Japanese law, and the application of contract law from each ASEAN country. The session on international trade law and international law on sale of goods was taught by professors from City University, UK. The session on the development of Japanese law was taught by professors from

---

* Kimpav is a manager of administration and law programs at the Faculty of Law and Public Affairs, PUC, and he attended the program with other students.

the KLS. To help understand the practice and development of Japanese law, the participants had a chance to visit the Yokohama Court and learn about the reform of the Japanese judicial system. As the last session of the program, students from each country gave a presentation on the application of the contract law of their country in the case of sales contracts. The presentation was also a platform for discussion and sharing different views on the application of laws and analysis.

2. In-Class Learning

2.1. World Trade Law

It was very interesting to learn about international trade law. This course covered the WTO system and its development for general understanding as well as some discussions on the GATT and dispute settlement. Cambodia has been a member of the WTO since 2004.[1] Students were asked how they would treat domestic products and imported products if their country was a member of the WTO. Students answered that they would support domestic products rather than imported products in order to promote local products. However, the correct response should have been that, as a member of the WTO, all the products must be treated equally without discrimination by consumers and state policies. Nevertheless, consumers may prefer domestic products, for example, because of the taste of the product.

On the subject of the GATT, the students were able to learn about the principles underlying it. The principles of non-discrimination on tariff policy by the state and state security or sovereignty were very important for the states. The non-discrimination on tariff policy has both pros and cons and sometime it depends on the state politics and bargaining power to be fair in trade negotiation. During the class, students discussed the issue of fairness for countries that import more and export less. Under the GATT, state members are required to limit the same rate of tariff in their policy and without discrimination. Therefore, large

---

[1] World Trade Organization, Cambodia and the WTO, see at https://www.wto.org/english/thewto_e/countries_e/cambodia_e.htm.

Class Session on International Sale of Goods (Trade Term and Case).

exporters may benefit more than importers.

As regards the Dispute Settlement Body of the WTO, the students learned about its functions and how this system works to settle disputes. This system is considered one of the most effective in dealing with trade disputes, especially in terms of the unequal treatment of the GATT and discrimination. During the class, the students also discussed the process and the effectiveness of this system for trade dispute settlement.

2.2. International Law on Sale of Goods

The students were taught about the common law system and how to find case law to provide them with a fundamental understanding of the system to help them easily understand international law on sale of goods. The key terms used in goods transactions and processes—including charter party, voyage charter, bill of landing, recap, and ex works, among others—were clearly explained in the class. This was new terminology for some students, though others were already familiar with the terms since they had previously practiced about or studied the subject. As regards the international sale of goods transactions, the students learned about the international laws that cover and relate to the area, such as UNCITRAL, the CISG, the Hague Rules, the Hague–Visby Rules, the Hamburg Rules, the Rotterdam Rules, and the CLC, among others. Understanding the processes of the international sale of goods was complicated for those students who had never had any practical experience of the subject. There are many processes and requirements that include clauses and contracts for the protection of the parties. Processes of international sale of goods include free along side ship, free on board, cost-insurance-freight, delivery at port, and delivery duty pay. In each process, there are different clauses and contracts and different parties involved. That is the reason why those students with no practical experience found it a bit complicated. However, the students learned a lot, and the class was vital for them.

2.3. The Development of Japanese Law

The students learned about the development of the Japanese Constitution and the impact of globalization on the amendment to the Civil Code of Japan on obligation, particularly the provisions on contract. About the Japanese Constitution, students were taught with discussion about the provisions on the military power in the Constitution. Japan used the referendum method to amend its constitution.

In the session on the amendment of the provisions on contract, the students learned the following points.

2.3.1. Reasons for the Change

- The change of the contractual principle from the Roman law and civil law principle of "impossibilium obligation [est]" to the common law principle of "obligation caused by contract shall be absolute."
- The change of the source of the binding force of contractual obligations from the general "rules" of the law to the "terms" of the contract.
- The change of the source of the obligation from the "fault" of the parties to the promise or assumption by the parties.

2.3.2. Background for the Change

The change was made because of the increasing influence of the movements in international law of trade such as the following:

- The United Nations Convention on Contracts for the International Sale of

Goods (CISG) 1980

- The Principles of European Contract Law (PECL), 1995, 1996, and 2010
- The Principles of International Commercial Contracts (PICC), 1994, 2004, and 2010
- The Principles, Definitions and Model Rules of European Private Law, Draft Common Framework of Reference (DCFR), 2009

2.3.3. Applicability of International Trade Rules to the Domestic Rules

Advantages

Unification of the domestic rules of different countries may facilitate reduction in various costs.…

Disadvantages

Rules that are convenient for business persons are not always kind and fair to the general public;…

To ensure that the students fully understood the application of the Civil Code of Japan on the provisions contract, two cases on sales contract were presented showing the application of these provisions before the amendment and after the amendment.

2.4. Trade Transaction (Role play)

Although less taxing for students, this method provided comprehensive knowledge regarding to the real trade transactions in the market. Some groups of student acted as companies with a lot of money, raw materials, and the tools to produce the products to sell on the market, while other groups acted as companies with shortages of resources and materials as well as tools. In this way, students learned different perspectives and how to negotiate with other groups (companies) to exchange products in order to increase their number of products on the market. As in the real market, the price of a product can go up and down, meaning that groups of students (companies) need to be smart in order to avoid losing profit. After the role play, students were asked for their feedback on what they had learned.

3. Visiting Yokohama Court

Students had the opportunity to explore and learn about the court system of Japan by visiting Yokohama Court. During the study visit, students met a judge at Yokohama Court, and he explained the Japanese court system and the current reforms.

The judge introduced the students to the hierarchy of the court. The Japanese court system consists of district courts, high courts, and the Supreme Court. In addition to these courts, there are also other special courts, such as the Property Court and the Intellectual Property Courts.

There are two mains reasons behind the current reform of the court system. The first reason is the criticism of the Japanese people, and the second reason is the need for more human resources to work in the courts. The reform is closely linked to legal education in Japan in order to produce competent students and to fill the need for human resources.

4. Comparison of Contract Law

To enable a comprehensive understanding of the law applied in contract, participating students from each country (Cambodia, Laos, Myanmar, and Vietnam) gave a presentation on how their home law is applied in contract cases. The below two sales contract cases were devised, and students were asked to prepare a presentation.

Case 1: Sales contract between A and B for the sale of oranges that was concluded before a typhoon hit A's orange farm. A is not able to deliver the oranges to B due to the damages to the farm caused by the typhoon. B had concluded a contract with C (a shop) for the supply of the oranges after concluding the contract with A. As a consequence, B would terminate the sales contract and claim compensation for damages.

PUC-FLPA students Presentation on Cambodia Law Apply in: case study of the sale contract.

Case 2: Sales contract between A and B for the sale of oranges that was concluded after a typhoon hit A's orange farm. A did not know that the farm had been damaged by the typhoon when he/she concluded the contract with B. Because of the serious damage to the farm, A is unable to deliver the oranges to B. B had concluded a contract with C (a shop) for the supply of the oranges after concluding the contract with A.

In the student presentations, there were differences in the laws that could be applied and differences in the conditions. There was a very useful discussion on force majeure since it was an important point in the sample cases. Cambodian and Japanese law (civil code) share similar provisions and can be applied similarly in these two cases. However, in Vietnam, there were different laws applicable in those two cases. Notably, Vietnamese law has a clear definition of force majeure and condition be considered, while the Civil Code of Cambodia is still vague on those points, though force majeure is explained in the glossary of the Code. For Myanmar, there were two laws applicable in the cases: the Sale of Goods Act (1930) and the Contract Act (1872). There was only one law on contract and tort that was applicable to the cases as presented by the students from Lao PDR.

5. Conclusion

As observed from the classes, it is notable that for general understanding, the lecture method is good for students since the professor plays an important role in leading students in the right direction. However, there was also participation from the students during the class on some particular issues and topics. It would be good if students were given the chance for more discussion in class as this can make the class more interesting. Case finding and reading was new to many of the participating students since they came from civil law systems and thus were not very familiar with this method. Role play, the study visit, and the students' presentations provided the opportunity for students to learn and reflect. During the study visit, the students had more of a chance to interact and ask more about practical issues. In the student presentations, all presenters shared a similar approach of applying the law to the cases; however, no case law was used. It is widely understood that accessing court decisions or case law in the participating students' countries is a challenge.

For future programs, it would be better to make the program more specific and more practical so that it can provide more chances for students to be more active in class and to gain more benefit from the program. This platform will bring students together to learn about and exchange ideas from different perspectives and experiences. The collaboration and supporting student to join together in such of this seminar/program is very significance that will enhance student more knowledge and experience from the seminar/program. The MOA just signed by the two institutions, KLS and PUC-FLPA, will provide more mutual benefits to the students from the KLS and PUC-FLPA as well as other partner universities of KLS. Therefore, making this program as a regular occurrence is important.

FROM LAW CLASSROOMS IN ASIAN UNIVERSITIES:

Short Report on the Collaboration Program
in Thailand

Hiroshi Matsuo* and Hitomi Fukasawa**

(Keio University Law School)

1. Introduction

From September 11 to 19, 2017, Keio University Law School (KLS: Tokyo Japan) conducted a Collaboration Program for Comparative Legal Education with the Thammasat University Faculty of Law (TU: Bangkok, Thailand). This Program consisted of (a) special lectures by Thai teachers and Japanese teachers on constitutional law and civil law, (b) presentations by Thai students and Japanese students on the common topic, and (c) participation in some normal classes. These joint classes were held at TU's Tha Phra Chan Campus in Bangkok. From KLS, 6 students (4 J.D. students and 2 LL.M. students) and 2 teachers (1 professor of civil law and 1 professor of constitutional law) participated. Around 30 Thai students and 10 teachers took part in the program.

KLS started the Collaboration Program in March 2017. In March 2017, KLS held a joint class with the Vietnam National University of Economics and Law (UEL: Ho Chi Minh City, Vietnam) and the Pannasastra University Cambodia, Faculty of Law and Public Administration (PUC-FLPA: Phnom Penh, Cambodia).[1]

---

* Professor of Law at KLS and the Director of Keio Institute for Global Law and Development (KEIGLAD: http://keiglad.keio.ac.jp/en/).

** Researcher of Law at Keio Institute for Global Law and Development (KEIGLAD).

[1] For details, see H. Matsuo and H. Fukasawa, "From Law Classrooms in Asian Universities: Short Report on the Collaboration program in Vietnam and Cambodia," *Comparative Legal*

The purposes of the Collaboration Program include making students experience the differences in legal education across universities in terms of content, materials, and pedagogical methods; deepening an understanding of various political, economic, and social backgrounds of those differences; and promoting further exchange of students and teachers for advancing the development of legal education at each of the participating universities.

The major components of the Collaboration Program have been (a) lectures by foreign teachers on current legal topics in their home country, (b) student presentations of their legal solutions, based on the application of their nation's laws, on a common topic provided to the students in advance, followed by questions and discussions, and (c) class observations by foreign students at the host university.

This program was implemented as a part of the Programs for Asian Global Legal Professions (PAGLEP) and was its second trial for holding joint classes to promote international exchange between the law students and teachers of different countries in Asia. It is worthwhile, we believe, to record our challenges and findings for the further development of the PAGLEP.

In this report, we will introduce the activities in the Collaboration Program at TU by focusing on the student presentations (the component (b) above) and the class observations (the component (c) above)3. Through the review of those activities, we attempt to draw some findings for improving legal education in Asian universities.[2]

Education from Asian Perspective, KEIGLAD, 2017, pp.157-174.

[2] As for the special lectures (as the component (a) above), two lectures in the public law field and the civil law field were provided from both side respectively. In the public law lectures, a Thai teacher talked on "The Current Issues in Thai Constitution Law" and a Japanese teacher lectured on "The Current Issues in Japanese Constitution Law." The recent movement in constitutional monarchy was one of the common interests.

In the civil law lectures, a Thai teacher lectured on "Fault in Thai Legal System" and a Japanese teacher talked on "Globalization Impacts on the Amendment to the Civil Code of Japan." One of the focal points was the responsibility of contracting parties for the loss caused by natural disasters which had not been attributable to both parties. Participants made questions and comments from the comparative point of view whether a debtor, without any

FROM LAW CLASSROOMS IN ASIAN UNIVERSITIES

2. Presentations and Discussions on the Common Topic

2.1 Common Topic

The below mentioned common topic assigned to the students was based on a case that had actually occurred in the recent past. It was provided to the participating students from Thailand and Japan in advance.

To compare students' analyses and discussions, we used almost the same case as was used in the Ho Chi Minh Program and the Phnom Penh Program in March, 2017.

The students were asked to analyze the question provided at the end of the topic and to suggest solutions by applying the laws of their own country.

Mr. A owns a piece of land and the building on it in Thailand/Japan. He lives in the U.K. and asked Ms. B to manage the land and the building. B lent the building to Company C as A's agent by concluding a lease contract. In that contract it was prescribed that the duration of the lease was 2 years; however, C may cancel the lease by providing a notice 3 months in advance or by paying the rent for 3 months before the expiration of the term. The rent was agreed to be USD 1000 per month and must be paid for one year in advance. C paid USD 12000 to B and began to possess the building, using it as office. After a year and a half has passed, B and C negotiated the renewal of the contract and agreed to continue the contract under the same terms except for the amount of the rent, which was to be USD 1200 per month.

At around the same time, A sold the land and the building to Company D. B was informed by A about the sale after C agreed to renew the contract with B, but B did not tell C. C paid B the new rent for one year (USD 14400) and continued to use the building. One month passed after the renewal of the contract between B and C, A and D registered the transfer of the title of the land and the building, and D notified C to vacate the build-

---

exemption clauses, could be exempted from the compensation for damages due to the impossibility to perform the contract or not.

ing. C informed B about it, but B responded that he was informed about the transfer of the land and building to D after the renewal of the lease contract. Then, B asked D to continue the lease contract and provided the rent that B had received from C (USD 14400). D received the rent but claimed that the rent should be USD 1500 per month and C should perform the additional payment of USD 3600. However, C refused to accept the increased rent. D brought the case to court, claiming that C should vacate the building. Should D's claim be recognized?

There are two main discussing points:

(1) Who were the parties to the lease contract that was concluded between B and C?

(2) Did the renewed contract between Ms. B and Company C succeed to Company D?

2.2 Presentation by Japanese Students

2.2.1 Analysis of Discussion Point (1)

For the Discussion point (1), the Japanese students faithfully analyzed the facts in accordance with legal syllogism.

They quoted Article 99 (1) of the Japanese Civil Code, which provides that a manifestation of intent made by an agent on behalf of the principal within the scope of the agent's authority binds the principal, and explained the requirements and effects of that provision. They divided the requirements of the provision into three elements: (1) an agent acted juristically with a third party; (2) the juristic act of the agent is "within the scope of the agent's authority," and (3) the agent represents "that the same is made on behalf of the principle" when performing the juristic act. The students concluded that the juristic act "binds the principle" if it is satisfies these three requirements stated above. They analyzed whether each element was satisfied one by one.

The interpretation of the requirements was also based on legal syllogism. When the students examined element (2) (whether the lease of the land and the

– 172 –

Common Topic Discussion with Thai and Japanese Students

building was "within the scope of the agent's authority"), they introduced two rules of interpretation. First, the scope of the agent's authority is judged through the reasonable interpretation of the content of the contract between the agent and the principal. Second, if there is no agreement on the scope of the agent's authority, Article 103 of Japanese Civil Code shall be applied. They mentioned that the second rule may apply to this case as the content of the contract between the agent and the principal was vague and they did not seem to have any agreement on the scope of the agent's authority. The students found that the second rule should apply, because A and B did not clearly agree that leasing the land and building was within B's authority. They quoted Article 103 of Japanese Civil Code, which provides that an agent who has no specified authority shall have the authority only to perform the following acts: (i) acts of preservation and (ii) acts with the purpose of using or improving any property or right that is the subject of the agency to the extent that such act does not change the nature of the property or right. They interpreted that the phrase, "*acts which have the purpose of using or improving any Thing ... to the extent such act does not change the nature of such property,*" ((ii) above) should include the act of making profit and applied it to the lease contract of land and building. The students concluded that B's juristic act satisfied the three requirements and bound A with C in accordance with Article 99 (1) of Japanese Civil Code Article 99. Their answer to the discussion point (1) was that the parties to the lease contract were A and C.

2.2.2 Analysis of Discussion Point (2)

For discussion point (2), the Japanese students explained the general rules governing lease contracts. The lease contract bound only A and C as the contracting parties, and it did not bind Company D, a third party, in this case. Therefore, in principle, D could vacate Company C from the land and the building on the grounds that D acquired ownership of the land and building, and D was not bound by the lease contract between A and C. Thus, C did not have any legal right to possess the land and building against D.

However, this rule was modified by a special law. Article 31 (1) of the Act on the Lease of Land and Building Leases provides that *"even if the building lease is not registered, at the time the buildings are delivered, the building lease shall subsequently become effective in respect to the person who has acquired real rights to said buildings."* The building was delivered to Company C before it was sold to Company D. Therefore, C could make a counterclaim that C had a legal right to continue possession of the building that was enforceable against D. Consequently, D could not vacate C from the land on which the building was constructed.[3]

To explain their result from this theoretical point of view, students analyzed whether a lease contract between Mr. A and Company C succeeded to Company D. They introduced a Japanese Supreme Court Precedent[4] on this point. According to the precedent, the original owner's legal status as a lessor shall be transferred to the new owner with the transfer of the ownership of the leased property. Students concluded that the renewed lease contract between Mr. A and Company C bound Company D. Therefore, Company D could neither increase the rent nor

---

[3] However, this rule is not specifically stipulated under any law. Instead, Article 10 of Act on the Lease of Land and Building provides that if Mr. A leased a piece of land to Company C, and C built itself a building on the land and registered ownership of the building in C's name, C could claim legal right to the land against Company D who bought and acquired ownership of the land from A.

[4] Japanese Supreme Court Judgment, April 23, 1971, Minshu Vol.25, No.3, at 388.

– 174 –

vacate C from the land and building.

2.3 Presentation by Thai Students
2.3.1 Analysis of Discussion Point (1)

The Thai student's presentation was also based on legal syllogism. First, they introduced the Thai Civil and Commercial Code. According to Article 797 and Article 820 of the Thai Civil and Commercial Code, Mr. A and Company C were the contracting parties to the lease contract because Ms. B concluded the lease contract as Mr. A's agent. Japanese students and Thai students reached the same conclusion on this point.

However, Thai students introduced a unique provision from the perspective of comparative law. If a principal has a domicile in a foreign country, the agent is personally liable for the contract even if the name of the principal has been disclosed (Article 824).[5] This is an exception to Article 820 of the Thai Civil and Commercial Code. The purpose of this Article is to protect the other party to a contract if the principal cannot promptly perform his/her responsibility outside the country. The students explained that Mr. A lived in the U.K. and did not have his domicile in Thailand. Therefore, Ms. B would be held liable for the contract. However, it was not clear whether both Mr. A and Ms. B were liable for the contract or if only B, as the agent, had the responsibility of the contract. The students referred to this matter in the discussion section.

2.3.2 Analysis of Discussion Point (2)

The ownership of immoveable property was transferred from Mr. A to Company D by agreement and registration in Thailand. According to Article 569 of the Thai Civil and Commercial Code,[6] in this case, the legal status of a lessor

---

[5] Article 824 of the Thai Civil and Commercial Code provides that an agent who makes a contract on behalf of a principal who is located and has his domicile in a foreign country is personally liable for the contract even though the name of the principal has been disclosed, unless the terms of the contract are inconsistent with his liability.

[6] Article 569 of Thai Civil and Commercial Code: A lease contract of immovable property is not extinguished by the transfer of ownership of the leased property. The transferee is enti-

shall be transferred to the new owner. However, to apply this provision, the lease contract must meet two requirements as provided under Article 538 of Thai Civil and Commercial Code.[7] First, the duration of the lease contract must be more than three years. Second, the lease contract should be formed by a formal (written) contract. The students explained that if the lessee, Company C, could establish that the lease agreement met these two requirements, C could claim the legal obligations passed to the new owner, Company D.

2.4 Discussions and Findings

2.4.1 Discussion of Discussion Point (1)

Thai students asked Japanese students the following questions: Under Japanese Civil Code, are both the principal, Mr. A, and his agent, Ms. B, liable under the lease contract? Does the Japanese Civil Code stipulate special provisions if the principal is domiciled abroad? These questions related to Article 824 of the Thai Civil and Commercial Code. Japanese students answered that under the provision of Japanese Civil Code, only the principal should be liable for a contract, and they could not find any special provision for cases in which the principal has domiciled abroad.

The teachers were also interested in Article 824. A Thai teacher, a moderator, confirmed the meaning of this provision by asking students whether Article 824 would presuppose that only an agent should be liable for the contract, or that both principal and agent should be liable. One male student answered that, following Article 820, Article 824 would not provide that a principal could be exempted from the obligations caused by a contract. It stipulates that an agent must also be liable for obligations under a contract if the principal has domiciled abroad. Under the rules of Article 820 and Article 824, both a principal and an agent are liable for the obligations under the contract, and the other party may

tled to the rights and is subjected to the duties of the transferor as the lessor.

[7] Article 538 of Thai Civil and Commercial Code: A lease of immovable property is not enforceable by action unless there is some written evidence signed by the party liable. If the lease is for more than three years or for the life of the lessor or lessee, it is enforceable only for three years unless it is made in writing and registered by the competent official.

make claims against both the principal and the agent.

Then, the discussion moved to the reason for Article 824. Other female students answered that it is meant to be beneficial for the other party to a contract because, if the principal were not in Thailand, the other party would not be able to make a timely claim for the performance of an obligation. However, the teacher kept asking all the students, "This is the *practical* reason. What is the *theoretical* reason for Article 824? Why should agent B be liable? B is not a party to the contract." The nature of the special liability imposed by law on an agent is analyzed by comparing it with the other types of liability imposed by law on a person who has a special relationship with the obligor.

2.4.2 Discussion of Discussion Point (2)

The interesting point was that both the Thai and Japanese students reached the same conclusion under the laws of their countries even though their approaches were different. The discussion was focused on the differences in legal reasoning.

First, both the Thai and Japanese students confirmed that ownership should be considered an absolute right. Thus, the new owner, Company D, could vacate C from the land based on its ownership, and C could not make a counterclaim that it had a right to possess the land based on the lease contract because the lease contract could bind only the parties. C's claim could be asserted only against the lessor, not against the new owner as a third party to the contract. Thus, "a sales contract ends a lease relationship" (*emptio tollit locatum*). This principle came from traditional Roman law; however, it was modified both in Thailand and Japan.

Under Thai law, Article 569 of the Thai Civil and Commercial Code provides that a lease contract does not end by transferring the ownership of immovable properties. Under Japanese law, the Act on the Protection of Building, Act on Land Lease, and Act on Building Lease were enacted, which were succeeded by the Act on Land and Building Lease. Article 31 (1) of the Act on Land and Building Lease provides that a lessee who had a building delivered to him/her before the ownership of the building was transferred to a third person can claim his/her

– 177 –

rights under the lease against the new owner. In addition, the Japanese Supreme Court held that the legal status of a lessor in a lease contract for immobile property shall be transferred to the new owner together with the ownership of that immovable property. This precedent was recognized by law through the amendment of the Japanese Civil Code in June, 2017, which added Article 605-2 to that effect. What is the difference between Thai law and Japanese law? The students discussed this point.

Japanese students explained that according to Article 31 (1) of the Act on Land and Building Lease, the right of lessee shall become effective against a new owner through the delivery of the buildings, and this rule could be recognized as an exception to the principle that "a sales contract ends a lease relationship." This provision does not change the right of lessee (a kind of claim right) into a real right that is effective against a third party; however, the right of lessee shall become similar to a real right through the effect of law, and the former lessor shall be succeeded by the new owner in the contractual relationship.

The Thai students explained that the transfer of immovable property could not be valid unless the sales contract had been concluded through a formal procedure, as provided by law, and the registration has been completed as required under Article 1299 of the Thai Civil and Commercial Code.[8] Under Thai law, a new owner shall succeed the previous owner in a lease contract through the change in ownership of a leased immovable property. One point of difference from the Japanese law is that the right of the lessee over the immovable property is recognized as neither a real right nor similar to a real right but just the legal status of a lessor caused by a change in the property's ownership.[9]

Last, the students discussed the reason that the Roman legal principle, "sale contract ends a lease relationship," was modified both in Thailand and Japan. It

---

[8] Article 1299 (1) of the Thai Civil and Commercial Code: Subject to a provision of this Code or other laws, no acquisition by juristic act of immovable or of real right appertaining thereto is complete unless the juristic act is made in writing and the acquisition is registered by the competent official.

[9] As a result of an amendment to Japanese Civil Code by adding Article 605-2, as stated above, a similar provision was introduced into Japanese law.

was indicated that the modifications aimed to increase the protection of the rights of the lessee and to reduce the instability of his/her legal status.

2.4.3 Findings

Through the discussion, the idea that a lessee should be guaranteed stable possession was found in both Thai and Japanese law, although the approach to reach this conclusion and the requirements for protecting the lessee were not always the same. The teachers indicated that there remained room to explain theoretically the protection of the lessee's interest through the doctrines even though it was already stipulated explicitly by the provision of law: that is, how to explain the reason why a sales contract (and a transfer of ownership) does *not* end a lease relationship by the proper use of doctrines.

3. Class Observations

The Japanese participants observed a tax law class and an insolvency law class at TU. Both classes were conducted in English.

3.1 Tax Law

3.1.1 General Information for the Class

The tax law class had more than 50 students. The majority of the students were Thai, however, some had also came from abroad. The teaching style was a lecture, and the teacher used detailed power point slides with figures, pictures, and tables in addition to handouts. The teacher had worked in a tax office, and has been teaching tax law as a part-time teacher.

3.1.2 Class Topic

The students studied personal income tax (PIT) computation and deemed income. First, the teacher explained the general rule to calculate tax. Gross income is multiplied by 0.055 percent, equal to the tax, and the standard income is calculated differently depending on whether the tax payer is an individual or

– 179 –

a household. After confirming the general information, he used cases to explain the typical types of calculations, for example, a case of a single person, a case of a married couple, and a case of a married couple with children. In this report, we will introduce the explanation about the case of the married couple.

The teacher explained how much tax the couple should pay when both the husband and the wife have been working. He gave students some basic information about the couple, including the income of the husband, the income of the wife, income level, deemed income, and number of children. Then, the students calculated the amount of tax owed using this information. In class, the teacher provided the answer using general information of the tax law.

According to the current tax law, the tax of the husband is calculated separately from the wife's income. However, in the past, around 50 years ago, the Thai Supreme Court Judgment held, based on its interpretation of the Thai Constitution, that the income of the wife was recognized as the income of her husband, and the total revenue of the couple was used as the basis for tax calculation. It seems that the current tax law violates the Constitution. However, under the current law, this judgment is considered to be one option for tax calculation. Both the joint calculation and the separate calculation are used in practice. The teacher explained the practical usage of the joint calculation and the process of filling out the application. In a case in which a couple owns a small business together, the joint calculation is used for tax calculation because it is hard to distinguish who is an employee and who is an employer. Another case in which the joint calculation was used was one where only the husband was working. In addition, this household would also get a spouse allowance. The teacher provided various cases and asked questions by changing the conditions, for example, a case in which the husband got a bonus or in which the tax documents of a single man were accepted as a document of single father with five children.

The class lasted three hours with one ten-minute break and most of the time was used for tax calculation. Compared with Japanese tax law courses, it seemed that the class focused on providing students with more practical knowledge and information necessary for a taxpayer.

3.2 Insolvency Law

3.2.1 General Information for the Class

Around 70 students attended the class on insolvency law. The teaching style was a lecture, and the teacher used power point slides that summarized principles and provided the provisions of laws and cases in addition to handouts.

3.2.2 The Class Topic

In the beginning of the class, the teacher reviewed what they learned last week, which was about the right and authority of the receiver[10] of the debtor's property. The rights of debtors shall be limited if a court orders receivership, and a receiver must be chosen (Article 22 and Article 24 of the Thai Bankruptcy Act). A receiver can seize a debtor's property (Article 19 of the Thai Bankruptcy Act); however, he cannot dispose of it, except for the properties in which the value goes down over time, until the court gives a judgment of bankruptcy.

The topic of the class was the interpretation of Article 22 of the Thai Bankruptcy Act.[11] This article stipulates that the authority of a receiver belongs exclusively to him/her. Article 22 (1) provides that *"to manage and dispose of the debtor's property"* is an authority of a receiver. The question for interpretation was the kind of action that should be recognized as *management and disposal of property*. First, the teacher asked students whether the receiver would be able to do the debtor's business. The answer was no, because doing business could not be recognized as the management and disposal of property.

As an example of the authority, a receiver could receive a payment from a

---

[10] In this section, a "receiver" is the administrator of a debtor's bankrupted property.

[11] Article 22: Upon the Court's receivership order against the debtor, the Receiver alone has the powers as follows:

(1) to manage and dispose of the debtor's property or to do such act as is necessary for the accomplishment of the debtor's unfinished business;

(2) to collect and receive money or property which will devolve upon the debtor or which the debtor is entitled to receive from other persons;

(3) to conclude a compromise or institute any action or defend any action in connection with the debtor's property.

Lecter of Insolvency Law

debtor of the insolvent (Article 22 (2)). The claim against the debtor should exist before the order of receivership. For example, Mr. A, a debtor, lent 200,000 baht to Ms. B. However, A became insolvent. Receivership was ordered by the court, and Ms. C was chosen to be the receiver. In this case, Ms. C can claim repayment to Ms. B.

The teacher moved to discuss Article 119. This article stipulates that a receiver can demand payment from the debtor of an insolvent. However, the insolvent's claim against the debtor should exist before the order of receivership. He asked students to consider the following case:

Case 1
Mr. A, a debtor, becomes insolvent. The court ordered receivership for A and chose Ms. B as a receiver. B signed a lease contract to lend A's property to Mr. K and delivered the property to K. However, K did not pay the fee for the lease. Can B bring a lawsuit against K claiming the payment of the fee on the basis of Article 119 of the Bankruptcy Act?

The teacher said that the claim was outside the scope of Article 119 because the lease of the property was made after the receivership was ordered. In this case, Mr. K is a debtor to Ms. B. Therefore, B could bring a lawsuit against K as his creditor.

FROM LAW CLASSROOMS IN ASIAN UNIVERSITIES

Next, the teacher explained what kind of cases could be covered by Article 22 (3) by using some fictional cases:

Case 2

Mr. A leased a house from Mr. K. However, A became insolvent and could not pay the fee under his lease contract with K. The court ordered receivership for A and chose Ms. B as the receiver. To whom can K bring his claim to vacate the house?

The teacher answered that K should claim and bring a lawsuit against A because the lawsuit is not concerned with the debtor's property. Case 2 was outside the scope of Article 22 (3) of the Bankruptcy Act.

Case3

Mr. A, a debtor, signed a contract with Mr. B to rent his car, and B delivered his car to A. However, A became insolvent, and the court ordered receivership and chose Mr. C as the receiver. B wants to terminate the lease contract and recover the car. Against whom can B make a claim for the return of his car? A or C?

The teacher answered that B can bring a lawsuit against A, the debtor, not C, the receiver, "because the car did not belong to A." Thus, Article 22 (3) of the Bankruptcy Act only allows the management of property which has "the relationship with debtor's property."

Using these cases, the teacher confirmed the interpretation of Article 22 of the Bankruptcy Act and emphasized its importance.

Next, the teacher moved to another topic related to the debt composition.[12] In Thai insolvency law, the composition must be approved prior to bankruptcy. Using the following example, he explained Article 56 of the Bankruptcy Act, which

---

[12] The composition of debt in this context means the readjustment of repayment by the negotiation between the debtor and the creditors for the reconstruction of the debtor's business.

is concerned with the effect of an order approving composition.

Case

In March 2016, Mr. A, a debtor, borrowed 1 million baht from Ms. B. In April, 2016, A borrowed 1 million baht from Mr. C. However, A became insolvent in June, then temporary receivership was ordered for A, and a receiver was chosen. Ms. D lent 1 million baht to A in July, 2016. In August, 2016, temporary receivership became absolute receivership. The composition started for A, and only creditor B submitted an application for the repayment of the debt. The court ordered an approval of composition, which said A should return 60% of his debt. Are C and D bound by the content of the composition or not?

According to the teacher's explanation, D was not bound by the composition because D lent money to A after the temporary receivership (Article 94). Only B and C were creditors who were bound by the composition in this case. Furthermore, who could receive a payment? The answer was B because only a creditor who submitted an application for repayment of debt could receive a payment from the composition (Article 91). However, B's credit was reduced to 600,000 baht due to the composition.

The lecture lasted around 3 hours with a ten-minute break, and students asked the teacher many questions after the class.

The teaching style was almost the same as that of the insolvency law classes in Japan. For example, Japanese teachers also use various cases to facilitate the understanding of provisions and the process of law. However, the teacher did not use actual cases or precedents in the class that we observed. We still need to learn more about the use of precedents in Thai legal education.

3.3 Conclusions on the Class Observations

It was our first time observing classes in Thailand. However, the students, in addition to the teachers, followed the lectures until the end. The reason seemed

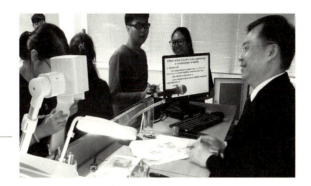

Teacher of Insolvency Law
Class Answers Students
Questions

to be that both lectures presented topics that are indispensable to daily life.

The tax law class was presented from the perspective of a taxpayer and focused on how we should pay taxes.

Insolvency law is recognized as an advanced legal subject in Japan because it is related to various fields of law, including civil law, civil procedure, civil enforcement, and labor law. It is hard for students to understand without concrete cases. However, by using examples, the teacher tried to make each legal issue as clear as possible.

Moreover, both classes were well designed for international students. We saw exchange students in both classes. By using power point slides, handouts, and many fictional cases, even international students who are not familiar with the Thai legal system could follow the classes. We were observers, and none of us knew Thai tax or insolvency law. However, after the class, we had begun to understand these laws.

From the perspective of comparative legal education, we think that the classes in Thailand were more focused on fostering human legal resources for daily life and business. The legal profession in Thailand is different from that in Japan. In Thailand, a legal license is required to represent a client in the court procedure. However, holding a bachelor's degree in law is enough to work as a legal consultant.

While in Japan, only those who have passed a bar examination or other legal professional exam can work as lawyers, and thus, an official license is essential.

Therefore, Japanese students are eager to study legal issues that are useful preparation for the bar exam. Notably, students in law schools are strongly demanding to absorb knowledge useful for the exam. Legal education in Japanese law school assumes how to solve the legal issues which are elaborated for the exam. In other words, teachers and students always consider how the case would be determined if it were brought to the court: how they would establish their argument, how they would collect the evidence, how they would find facts, and what Supreme Court precedent impacts their case.

It is not an issue of which educational model is better. We would like to find the reasons for their differences. We can conclude that the legal education methods are inseparable from the purpose of human resource development in each country's legal field. Before we design a teaching style, we need to make clear what type of human resources we would like to foster. If we train legal professions, we need to make it clear what legal professions are expected to do in society. Legal education methods depend on that answer.

We think that the ways in which legal professionals are certified influence the differences in legal education. In Thailand, the graduates of the faculty of law can provide legal consultation, although they cannot represent clients in the court unless they pass the bar exam, while in Japan only the lawyers who pass the state examination can provide any legal services. Which system better promotes access to justice? It is not for us to decide.

4. Conclusion

4.1 Legal Education Depends on the Social Expectations about the Legal Profession

As previously mentioned, the Collaboration Program at Thammasat University (TU) in Bangkok held in September, 2017, adopted the same framework as that conducted in Ho Chi Minh and Phnom Penh in March, 2017,[13] which consisted of (a) special lectures by teachers on current legal issues in each home

---

[13] See 1 above.

country, (b) presentations by students on the common topic, and (c) class observations at the host university. The purpose of using the same framework was to improve each component. For instance, we used the same "Common Topic" for the students' presentations and discussions because it enabled us to compare the characteristics of students' approaches to solve legal issues and to analyze the reasons for their similarities and differences, which will lead to the improvement of the cooperation programs and the development of common materials to be used among partner universities.

We made many findings during Bangkok Program. Students at TU naturally used legal syllogism to solve the legal issues included in the Common Topic, just like the students in Ho Chi Minh and Phnom Penh. Further, when they interpreted the law to apply it to the case, they always referred to the purpose of that law, as was illustrated previously in the students' interpretation of Article 820 of the Thai Civil and Commercial Code.[14] Teachers also frequently confirmed the reasons for the provision and asked students to discuss the law's theoretical justification. This may be a characteristic of the Thai legal education system.

There must be reasons for this pedagogical style. It seemed to be closely related with the system of the legal profession in Thailand, where the graduates of the faculty of law are able to provide legal consultation to their client regardless of licensing.[15] During legal consultation, clients often like to know not only the expected results of the legal conflict they are facing, but also the justification for the results based on a reasonable interpretation and application of laws. To answer these clients' queries, it would not be enough to merely identify the applicable laws. The pedagogical style that trains students to always think about the reason and theoretical justification for the law seems to be closely related with the social expectations for the legal professionals. It would be those fundamental social demands that determine a basic condition to developing legal professions, which will influence the teaching method of teachers and learning style of students.

---

[14] See 2.3.1 above.

[15] See 3.3 above.

In the rapidly globalizing Asian market, new and complicated legal conflicts are emerging, which cannot be easily solved through the simple application of existing laws. The PAGLEP aims to foster legal professionals who will tackle these unknown and difficult problems. The Bangkok Program gave us useful findings for the further development of the PAGLEP.

4.2 Dynamic Changes in Legal Education in Accordance with Development

There is no single, static, or ideal legal education system. It is always dynamically changing in accordance with the shifting social needs of each country.[16] As we have observed in the Ho Chi Minh Program, the Phnom Penh Program, and the Bangkok Program, the social needs for legal professionals were not identical. In the construction of a basic structure of the rule of law, the priority of the pedagogical method of legal education should be to the precise confirmation of black-letter law to be applied to the case. It is not easy for government officials or citizens to identify the proper provisions from the accumulation of overlapping laws and regulations to apply in a given circumstance. In this situation, legal professionals are expected to draw appropriate laws and regulations and to apply them to the case for the fair solution of the conflict. However, the role of legal professionals should change in accordance with the changes in the legal system of the country as a result of political and economic shifts. In accordance with the gradual legalization of a society, legal professionals will be often asked to explain the reasonable justification of laws, regulations or judgments. In this circumstance, even the increase of explicit legislation of congress, administrative regulation, and the judgement of court will not liberate legal professionals from their responsibility to explain the reason why the laws, regulations, and judgments should be or should not be justified to the citizen. It is evident, particularly

---

[16] In this situation, we want to know "what changes in society are related with what pedagogical aspects of legal education." See Hiroshi Matsuo, "Why and How Should Comparative Legal Education Be Promoted in an Asian Context," in: KEIGLAD, *Comparative Legal Education from Asian Perspective*, Keio University Press, 2017, p. 11.

– 188 –

FROM LAW CLASSROOMS IN ASIAN UNIVERSITIES

from the dynamically changing social context in Asia, that legal education must flexibly follow the changes in social needs for legal professions in each country.

MATERIAL

COURSE CATALOGS

COURSE CATALOGS: HANOI LAW UNIVERSITY

HANOI LAW UNIVERSITY, VIETNAM

Bachelor of Laws (LL.B.) Program

1) GENERAL EDUCATION (required course load 26 credits, excluding physical and military education)

1-1) Compulsory Courses (required course load: 22 credits)		
1-1-1) Basic Principles of Marxism - Leninism (1)	2 credits	Fall
1-1-2) Basic Principles of Marxism - Leninism (2)	3 credits	Fall
1-1-3) Ho Chi Minh Thought	2 credits	Spring
1-1-4) Revolution Lines of Vietnam Communist Party	3 credits	Spring
1-1-5) Sociology of Law	3 credits	Spring
1-1-6) Foreign Language (1) (choose 1 of the Languages: English, Russian, French, Chinese, Japanese, German), Legal Vietnamese (applying for foreign students)	3 credits	Fall / Spring
1-1-7) Foreign Language (2) (choose 1 of the languages: English, Russian, French, Chinese, Japanese, German), Legal Vietnamese (applying for foreign students)	4 credits	Fall / Spring
1-1-8) Informatics	2 credits	Spring
1-2) Elective Courses (required course load: 4 credits)		
1-2-1) Macroeconomics	2 credits	Fall / Spring
1-2-2) International Economic Relations	2 credits	Fall / Spring
1-2-3) History of World Civilisation	2 credits	Fall / Spring
1-2-4) General Vietnamese Culture	2credits	Fall / Spring
1-2-5) General Psychology	2credits	Fall / Spring

1-2-6) General Logic	2 credits	Fall / Spring
1-2-7) Legal Profession and Methods to Study Law	2 credits	Spring

2) PROFESSIONAL EDUCATION (required course load: 90 credits)

2-1) Compulsory Courses (required course load: 66 credits)		
2-1-1) Theory of State and Law	5 credits	Fall
2-1-2) Constitutional Law	4 credits	Fall
2-1-3) Legal Drafting	3 credits	Fall / Spring
2-1-4) Administrative Law	4 credits	Spring
2-1-5) Criminal Law (1)	3 credits	Spring
2-1-6) Criminal Law (2)	3 credits	Fall
2-1-7) Criminal Procedure Law	3 credits	Fall
2-1-8) Civil Law (1)	3 credits	Fall
2-1-9) Civil Law (2)	3 credits	Spring
2-1-10) Law on Marriage and Family	3 credits	Fall
2-1-11) Civil Procedure Law	3 credits	Spring
2-1-12) Commercial Law (1)	3 credits	Fall
2-1-13) Commercial Law (2)	3 credits	Spring
2-1-14) Labour Law	3 credits	Fall
2-1-15) Financial Law	3 credits	Fall
2-1-16) Land Law	3 credits	Spring
2-1-17) Public International Law	4 credits	Fall
2-1-18) Private International Law	4 credits	Spring
2-1-19) Law on ASEAN Community	3 credits	Spring

COURSE CATALOGS: HANOI LAW UNIVERSITY

2-1-20) International Trade Law	3 credits	Spring
2-2) Elective Courses (required course load: 24 credits)		
2-2-1) History of State and Law	3 credits	Spring
2-2-2) Comparative Law	3 credits	Spring
2-2-3) Organisation and Operation of the People's Courts and the People's Procuracies	2 credits	Fall / Spring
2-2-4) Foreign Constitutional Law	2 credits	Spring
2-2-5) Administrative Procedure Law	2 credits	Spring
2-2-6) Lawyering, Notarization and Certification	2 credits	Fall
2-2-7) Inspection and Handling of Complaints and Denunciations	2 credits	Spring
2-2-8) International Criminal Law	2 credits	Fall / Spring
2-2-9) Mafia Criminal Organization	2 credits	Fall / Spring
2-2-10) Criminology	2 credits	Fall / Spring
2-2-11) Criminal Investigation Science	2 credits	Spring
2-2-12) Special Criminal Procedure	2 credits	Spring
2-2-13) Judicial Psychology	2 credits	Spring
2-2-14) Law on Anti-corruption	2 credits	Spring
2-2-15) Intellectual Property Law	3 credits	Fall / Spring
2-2-16) Law on Secured Transactions	2 credits	Fall / Spring
2-2-17) Roman Law	2 credits	Spring
2-2-18) Law on Gender Equality	2 credits	Spring
2-2-19) Civil Matter Resolution Procedure	2 credits	Fall / Spring
2-2-20) Law on Enforcement of Civil Judgments	2 credits	Spring

2-2-21) Investment Law	2 credits	Fall / Spring
2-2-22) Social Security Law	2 credits	Fall / Spring
2-2-23) Insurance Business Law	2 credits	Fall / Spring
2-2-24) Competition Law and Consumer Protection Law	3 credits	Fall / Spring
2-2-25) Environmental Law	3 credits	Fall / Spring
2-2-26) Environmental Law in Business Activities	2 credits	Fall / Spring
2-2-27) Law on Real Estate Business	2 credits	Fall / Spring
2-2-28) Law on Compensation for Ground Clearance	2 credits	Fall / Spring
2-2-29) Law on People with Disabilities	2 credits	Fall / Spring
2-2-30) Modern International Law of the Sea	3 credits	Spring
2-2-31) Vietnamese Law and International Law on Human Rights	3 credits	Spring
2-2-32) Law on International Treaties	2 credits	Spring
2-2-33) Law on Tendering	2 credits	Fall / Spring
2-2-34) International Maritime Law	2 credits	Fall / Spring
2-2-35) International Law on Aviation Transportation	2 credits	Fall / Spring
2-2-36) International Commercial Arbitration Law	2 credits	Fall / Spring
2-2-37) Customs Law	2 credits	Fall / Spring
2-2-38) Law on European Union	3 credits	Spring
2-2-39) General Skills for Law Consultation	2 credits	Fall / Spring
2-2-40) Skills for Drafting Common Administrative Documents	2 credits	Fall / Spring

COURSE CATALOGS: HANOI LAW UNIVERSITY

2-2-41) Skills for Appraising Legal Normative Documents	2 credits	Fall / Spring
2-2-42) Law Consultation Skills for Administrative Law Related Matters	2 credits	Fall / Spring
2-2-43) Law Consultation Skills for Criminal Law Related Matters	2 credits	Fall / Spring
2-2-44) Law Consultation Skills for Civil Law Related Matters	2 credits	Fall / Spring
2-2-45) Law Consultation Skills for Marriage and Family Law Related Matters	2 credits	Fall / Spring
2-2-46) Law Consultation Skills for Intellectual Property Law Related Matters	2 credits	Fall / Spring
2-2-47) Law Consultation Skills for Commercial Law Related Matters	2 credits	Fall / Spring
2-2-48) Law Consultation Skills for Labour Law Related Matters	2 credits	Fall / Spring
2-2-49) Law Consultation Skills for Land Law Related Matters	2 credits	Fall / Spring
2-2-50) Law Consultation Skills for Tax and Enterprise Finance Related Matters	2 credits	Fall / Spring
2-2-51) Skills for Negotiation, Drafting and Implementation Of Contracts	2 credits	Fall / Spring
2-2-52) Skills for Participation in Resolution of Administrative Cases	2 credits	Fall / Spring
2-2-53) Skills for Practice of Some Activities in Criminal Procedure	2 credits	Fall / Spring
2-2-54) Skills for Participation in Resolution of Civil Cases	2 credits	Fall / Spring
2-2-55) [course taught in English] Introduction to the Vietnamese Legal System	2 credits	Fall

2-2-56) [course taught in English] Organization and Operation of the Judicial Organs in Vietnam	2 credits	Spring
2-2-57) [course taught in English] Modern Constitutionalism	2 credits	Spring
2-2-58) [course taught in English] Fundamental Civil Rights in the Modern World	2 credits	Spring
2-2-59) [course taught in English] Comparative Contract Law	2 credits	Fall
2-2-60) [course taught in English] WTO Law	2 credits	Spring
2-2-61) [course taught in English] International Investment Law	2 credits	Fall
2-2-62) [course taught in English] Law on International Franchising	2 credits	Spring
2-2-63) [course taught in English] Legal Reasoning and Legal Writing for Legal Professionals	2 credits	Fall
2-2-64) [course taught in English] Lawyers' Presentation Skills	2 credits	Spring

2-3) Thesis Writing; Professional Internship; and Enrollment of Other Professional Courses (required course load: 10 credits)

2-3-1) Thesis Writing: Applying for Students Meeting Conditions in Accordance with University's Regulations	10 credits	Fall / Spring

2-3-2) Students who do not meet conditions for thesis writing or do not choose to write thesis, must choose one of the following ways:

(i) Enrollment of Other Professional Courses: 10 credits; or

(ii) Doing professional Internship: 4 credits (equivalent to 180 internship hours in some agencies) and Enrollment of Other Professional Courses: 6 credits

Note:
Duration of the Program: 4 years (full-time)
* Course load: 120 credits (excluding physical and military education)

COURSE CATALOGS: UNIVERSITY OF ECONOMICS AND LAW HOCHIMINH CITY

UNIVERSITY OF ECONOMICS AND LAW, VIETNAM NATIONAL UNIVERSITY, HOCHIMINH CITY

LL.M. Program with Research Orientation

1) General Knowledge		
Philosophy	4 credits	Semester 1
2) Basic and Specialized Knowledge		
2-1) Compulsory courses		
2-1-1) Legal Research	2 credits	Semester 1
2-1-2) Property Law	3 credits	Semester 1
2-1-3) Enterprise Law	3 credits	Semester 1
2-1-4) Contract Law	3 credits	Semester 1
2-1-5) Commercial Law	3 credits	Semester 2
2-2) Optional Courses		
2-2-1) Law and Economics	2 credits	Semester 3
2-2-2) Competition Law	2 credits	Semester 2
2-2-3) Banking Law	2 credits	Semester 2
2-2-4) Dispute Settlement in Trade	2 credits	Semester 2
2-2-5) Intellectual Property Law	3 credits	Semester 2
2-2-6) Investment Law	2 credits	Semester 3
2-2-7) Environment Law	2 credits	Semester 2
2-2-8) Law on Bidding	2 credits	Semester 3
2-2-9) Tax Law on Business Activities	2 credits	Semester 2
2-2-10) Law on Accounting and Audit	2 credits	Semester 3

2-2-11) Law on Management of Foreign Currency and Monetary Market	2 credits	Semester 3
2-2-12) Merger and Acquisition	2 credits	Semester 3
2-2-13) Insurance Law on Business Activities	2 credits	Semester 3
2-2-14) Competition Procedure	2 credits	Semester 3
2-2-15) International Trade Law	3 credits	Semester 3
2-2-16) Law on Land and Real Estate Trading	3 credits	Semester 3
3) Master Thesis	15 credits	Semester 4

LL.M. Program with Practical Orientation

1) General Knowledge		
Philosophy	4 credits	Semester 1
2) Basic and Specialized Knowledge		
2-1) Compulsory Courses		
2-1-1) Legal Research	2 credits	Semester 1
2-1-2) Property Law	3 credits	Semester 1
2-1-3) Enterprise Law	3 credits	Semester 1
2-1-4) Contract Law	3 credits	Semester 1
2-1-5) Commercial Law	3 credits	Semester 2
2-2) Optional Courses		
2-2-1) Law and Economics	2 credits	Semester 3
2-2-2) Competition Law	2 credits	Semester 3
2-2-3) Banking Law	2 credits	Semester 2
2-2-4) Dispute Settlement in Trade	2 credits	Semester 2

COURSE CATALOGS: UNIVERSITY OF ECONOMICS AND LAW HOCHIMINH CITY

2-2-5) Intellectual Property Law	3 credits	Semester 2
2-2-6) Investment Law	2 credits	Semester 3
2-2-7) Environment Law	2 credits	Semester 2
2-2-8) Law on Bidding	2 credits	Semester 3
2-2-9) Tax Law on Business Activities	2 credits	Semester 2
2-2-10) Law on Accounting and Audit	2 credits	Semester 3
2-2-11) Law on Management of Foreign Currency and Monetary Market	2 credits	Semester 3
2-2-12) Merger and Acquisition	2 credits	Semester 3
2-2-13) Insurance Law on Business Activities	2 credits	Semester 3
2-2-14) Competition Procedure	2 credits	Semester 3
2-2-15) International Trade Law	3 credits	Semester 3
2-2-16) Law on Land and Real Estate Trading	3 credits	Semester 3
3) Master Thesis	7 credits	Semester 4

LL.B. Program

1) Basic Knowledge (general education): 36 credits

1-1) Compulsory Courses (25 credits)		
1-1-1) Basic Principles of Marxism – Leninism	5 credits	Semester 1
1) Revolutionary Guidelines of Vietnamese Communist Party	3 credits	Semester 3
2) Ho Chi Minh Thoughts	2 credits	Semester 2
3) Microeconomic 1	3 credits	Semester 1
4) Macroeconomic 1	3 credits	Semester 2
5) Introduction to State and Law	3 credits	Semester 1
6) Enterprise Law	3 credits	Semester 3
7) Basic Administration	3 credits	Semester 1
1-2) Optional Courses (11 credits)		
Group 1		
1) Psychology	3 credits	Semester 1
2) Introduction to Communication Science	3 credits	Semester 1
Group 2		
1) Applied Informatics Technology	2 credits	Semester 3
2) Logics	2 credits	Semester 3
Group 3		
1) International Relations	3 credits	Semester 2
2) Geopolitics	3 credits	Semester 2
Group 4		
1) Sociology	2 credits	Semester 2
2) Cultural Studies	2 credits	Semester 2

COURSE CATALOGS: UNIVERSITY OF ECONOMICS AND LAW HOCHIMINH CITY

Group 5		
1) Legal Research skills	2 credits	Semester 3
2) Team-work skills	2 credits	Semester 3

2) Specialized knowledge: 95 credits

2-1) Basic legal studies: 30 credits		
1) Tort Law	3 credits	Semester 4
2) Constitution	3 credits	Semester 2
3) Contract Law	3 credits	Semester 3
4) Civil Procedure	3 credits	Semester 5
5) History of State and Law in Viet Nam	3 credits	Semester 2
6) Introduction to Civil Law	3 credits	Semester 2
7) Property Law	3 credits	Semester 3
8) Administrative law	3 credits	Semester 3
9) Criminal Law	3 credits	Semester 5
10) Environment Law	3 credits	Semester 7
2-2) Specialized Legal Studies of Major: 55 credits		
2-2-1) Basic Knowledge of Major: 28 credits		
A) Compulsory Courses (21 credits)		
1) Intellectual Property Law	3 credits	Semester 7
2) Commercial Law	3 credits	Semester 4
3) Labour Law	3 credits	Semester 6
4) General contracts	3 credits	Semester 4
5) Criminal Procedure	3 credits	Semester 6
6) Tax Law	3 credits	Semester 6

– 203 –

7) Land Law	3 credits	Semester 4
B) Optional Courses (7 credits)		
1) Logistics	3 credits	Semester 4
2) International Trade Norms	2 credits	Semester 5
3) International Law of the Sea	2 credits	Semester 5
4) International Insurance Law	3 credits	Semester 5
5) International Aviation Law	2 credits	Semester 4

2-2-2) Specialized knowledge of major: 27 credits

A) Compulsory courses (21 credits)		
1) International Public Law	3 credits	Semester 4
2) Competition Law	3 credits	Semester 5
3) International Sales Law	3 credits	Semester 6
4) International Private Law	3 credits	Semester 5
5) Maritime Law	2 credits	Semester 6
6) Law of the World Trade Organization	3 credits	Semester 5
7) Banking Law	2 credits	Semester 7
8) Contract Negotiation and Drafting Skills	2 credits	Semester 7
B) Optional courses (6 credits)		
1) WTO Dispute Settlement Mechanism	2 credits	Semester 6
2) Trade Remedies	2 credits	Semester 6
3) Arbitration in International Trade	2 credits	Semester 6
4) Non-Tariff Barriers on Trade	2 credits	Semester 6

2-3) Internship and Dissertation: 10 credits

A) Compulsory courses: 4 credits

COURSE CATALOGS: UNIVERSITY OF ECONOMICS AND LAW HOCHIMINH CITY

Internship	4 credits	Semester 7
B) Optional courses: 6 credits (Dissertation or Specialized Subjects)		
Option 1: Dissertation	6 credits	Semester 7
Option 2: Specialized Subjects		
Subject 1: Custom Law	3 credits	Semester 7
Subject 2: Regulations on Insurance Trading	3 credits	Semester 7

Note:
Semester 1, 3, 5 and 7 start from September and end in December.
Semester 2, 4, 6 and 8 start from January and end in May.
1st grade students take the Semester 1 and 2, and 2nd grade students take the Semester 3 and 4.
3rd grade students take the Semester 5 and 6, and 4th grade students take the Semester 7 and 8.

PAÑÑĀSĀSTRA UNIVERSITY OF CAMBODIA
Faculty of Law and Public Affairs

LL.M. in IBL

YEAR I:

Foundation Year Courses	
2-1) Global Environment Awareness	3 credits
2-2) Fundamentals of Economics	3 credits
2-3) Negotiations and Conflict Resolutions	3 credits
4-4) Cambodian Laws in Context	3 credits
2-5) Introduction to International Law and Human Rights Law	3 credits
2-6) Advanced Legal Research and Writing	3 credits

YEAR II:

Basic Major Courses	
2-7) International Human Rights Law and Practice	3 credits
2-8) Business Law and Practice	3 credits
2-9) Intellectual Property Law and Practice	3 credits
Major Courses: International Business Law	
2-10) Advanced Labor Law	3 credits
2-11) International Trade Law	3 credits
2-12) International Commercial Dispute Settlement	3 credits
2-13) Advanced Corporation Law	3 credits
2-14) Advanced Law on Business Contracts	3 credits

COURSE CATALOGS: PAÑÑĀSĀSTRA UNIVERSITY OF CAMBODIA

Elective Courses (6 credits)	
2-15) Constitutional Rights: In a Comparative Perspectives	3 credits
2-16) Human Rights and Good Governance	3 credits
2-17) Governance, Management and Leadership Dynamics	3 credits
2-18) Human Rights and Business	3 credits
2-19) International Criminal Law	3 credits
2-20) Human Rights and Intellectual Property	3 credits
2-21) Advanced Taxation Law	3 credits
2-22) Competition and Consumer Law	3 credits
2-23) Securities Law	3 credits
2-24) Advanced Banking Law	3 credits
2-25) Comparative Insurance Law	3 credits
2-26) Globalization and Conflict of Law	3 credits
2-27) Human Rights and Labour Rights	3 credits
2-28) Human Rights and Mediation	3 credits
2-29) Moot Court Course	3 credits
2-30) Human Values Education	3 credits
2-31) Human Rights in South East Asia	3 credits
Graduation Paths*(choose one)	
Comprehensive Examination (2 seminars)	
2-32) Seminar in Public Law	3 credits
2-33) Seminar in Private Law	3 credits
2-34) Seminar in International Law	3 credits

Project Report Path	
2-35) Report and Thesis Research Methodologies and Writing	3 credits
2-36) Applied Report and Defence	3 credits
Thesis Path	
2-37) Report and Thesis Research Methodologies and Writing	3 credits
2-38) Master's Thesis	3 credits

Note:

PUC Academic Calendar [Nov-Apr: 9 credits], [Apr-Aug: 9 credits] and [Aug-Nov: 6 credits]

* Master of Law in International Business Law: 54 credits (18 courses)

LL.M. in IPL

YEAR I:

Foundation Year Courses	
3-1) Global Environment Awareness	3 credits
3-2) Fundamentals of Economics	3 credits
3-3) Negotiations and Conflict Resolutions	3 credits
3-4) Cambodian Laws in Context	3 credits
3-5) Introduction to International Law and Human Rights Law	3 credits
3-6) Advanced Legal Research and Writing	3 credits

YEAR II:

Basic Major Courses	
3-7) International Human Rights Law and Practice	3 credits
8-8) Business Law and Practice	3 credits
3-9) Intellectual Property Law and Practice	3 credits

Major Courses: Intellectual Property Law	
3-10) International Intellectual Property Law	3 credits
3-11) Copyright and Related Rights	3 credits
3-12) Trade Marks, Domain Names and Geographical Indications	3 credits
3-13) Patents, Utility Models and Trade Secrets	3 credits
3-14) Industrial Designs and Plant Variety Protection	3 credits
Elective Courses (6 credits)	
3-15) Constitutional Rights: In a Comparative Perspectives	3 credits
3-16) Human Rights and Good Governance	3 credits
3-17) Governance, Management and Leadership Dynamics	3 credits
3-18) Human Rights and Business	3 credits
3-19) International Criminal Law	3 credits
3-20) Human Rights and Intellectual Property	3 credits
3-21) Advanced Taxation Law	3 credits
3-22) Competition and Consumer Law	3 credits
3-23) Securities Law	3 credits
3-24) Advanced Banking Law	3 credits
3-25) Comparative Insurance Law	3 credits
3-26) Globalization and Conflict of Law	3 credits
3-27) Human Rights and Labour Rights	3 credits
3-28) Human Rights and Mediation	3 credits
3-29) Moot Court Course	3 credits

3-30) Human Values Education	3 credits
3-31) Human Rights in South East Asia	3 credits
Graduation Paths*(choose one)	
Comprehensive Examination (2 seminars)	
3-32) Seminar in Public Law	3 credits
3-33) Seminar in Private Law	3 credits
3-34) Seminar in International Law	3 credits
Project Report Path	
3-35) Report and Thesis Research Methodologies and Writing	3 credits
3-36) Applied Report and Defence	3 credits
Thesis Path	
3-37) Report and Thesis Research Methodologies and Writing	3 credits
3-38) Master's Thesis	3 credits

Note:
PUC Academic Calendar [Nov-Apr: 9 credits], [Apr-Aug: 9 credits] and [Aug-Nov: 6 credits]
* Master of Law in Intellectual Property Law: 54 credits (18 courses)

LL.M. in IHRL

YEAR I:

Foundation Year Courses	
4-1) Global Environment Awareness	3 credits
4-2) Fundamentals of Economics	3 credits
4-3) Negotiations and Conflict Resolutions	3 credits
4-4) Cambodian Laws in Context	3 credits
4-5) Introduction to International Law and Human Rights Law	3 credits

COURSE CATALOGS: PAÑÑĀSĀSTRA UNIVERSITY OF CAMBODIA

4-6) Advanced Legal Research and Writing	3 credits

YEAR II:

Basic Major Courses	
4-7) International Human Rights Law and Practice	3 credits
4-8) Business Law and Practice	3 credits
4-9) Intellectual Property Law and Practice	3 credits

Major Courses: International Human Rights Law	
4-10) Methods of Human Right Research (External Lecturer)	3 credits
4-11) International and Regional Human Right Laws	3 credits
4-12) Human Rights and Criminal Justice	3 credits
4-13) Contemporary Human Right Issues	3 credits
4-14) Human Rights and Women	3 credits

Elective Courses (6 credits)	
4-15) Constitutional Rights: In a Comparative Perspectives	3 credits
4-16) Human Rights and Good Governance	3 credits
4-17) Governance, Management and Leadership Dynamics	3 credits
4-18) Human Rights and Business	3 credits
4-19) International Criminal Law	3 credits
4-20) Human Rights and Intellectual Property	3 credits
4-21) Advanced Taxation Law	3 credits
4-22) Competition and Consumer Law	3 credits
4-23) Securities Law	3 credits

– 211 –

4-24) Advanced Banking Law	3 credits
4-25) Comparative Insurance Law	3 credits
4-26) Globalization and Conflict of Law	3 credits
4-27) Human Rights and Labour Rights	3 credits
4-28) Human Rights and Mediation	3 credits
4-29) Moot Court Course	3 credits
4-30) Human Values Education	3 credits
4-31) Human Rights in South East Asia	3 credits
Graduation Paths*(choose one)	
Project Report Path	
4-32) Report and Thesis Research Methodologies and Writing	3 credits
4-33) Applied Report and Defence	3 credits
Master's Thesis Path	
4-34) Report and Thesis Research Methodologies and Writing	3 credits
4-35) Master's Thesis	3 credits

Note:
PUC Academic Calendar [Nov-Apr: 9 credits], [Apr-Aug: 9 credits] and [Aug-Nov: 6 credits]
* Master of Law in International Human Rights Law: 54 credits (18 courses)

COURSE CATALOGS: PAÑÑĀSĀSTRA UNIVERSITY OF CAMBODIA

LL.B.

YEAR I:

Foundation Year Courses	
1-1) English I: Reading and Composition	3 credits
1-2) English II: Intermediate Reading and Composition	3 credits
1-3) Cultural Anthropology	3 credits
1-4) Introduction to Computers	4 credits
1-5) Environmental Science	3 credits
1-6) Introduction to Political Science	3 credits
1-7) Gender Studies	3 credits
1-8) Khmer Studies	3 credits
Oriented Courses	
1-9) Introduction to Law	3 credits
1-10) Basic Legal Concepts	3 credits

YEAR II:

Functional Skill Courses	
1-11) College Algebra	3 credits
1-12) Logic and Critical Thinking	3 credits
1-13) Academic Research-Information Literacy	3 credits
1-14) Introduction to Ethics	3 credits
1-15) Personal Growth and Development	3 credits
1-16) Health Education and Fitness	3 credits
1-17) Civil Law I: Family Law and Succession	3 credits
1-18) Business Law	3 credits

– 213 –

Oriented Courses	
1-19) Cambodian Constitution	3 credits
1-20) History of Cambodia	3 credits
1-21) ASEAN Governments, Politics and Economics	3 credits

YEAR III:

Basic Major Course	
1-22) Criminal Law (Substantives)	3 credits
1-23) Legal Research and Writing Skills	3 credits
1-24) Introduction to International Law	3 credits
1-25) Introduction to Public Policy and Administration	3 credits
1-26) Administrative Law	3 credits
1-27) Civil Law II (Property Law: Real Rights and Claims)	3 credits
1-28) Alternative Dispute Resolution (ADR)	3 credits
1-29) Civil Procedure	3 credits
1-30) Criminal Procedure	3 credits
1-31) Civil Law III (Obligation: Contract and Tort)	3 credits
1-32) Labor Law	3 credits

YEAR IV:

Major Courses	
1-33) Fiscal Legislation and Taxation	3 credits
1-34) International Human Rights Law	3 credits
1-35) Intellectual Property Law	3 credits

COURSE CATALOGS: PAÑÑĀSĀSTRA UNIVERSITY OF CAMBODIA

1-36) Legal Systems of ASEAN Nations	3 credits
1-37) Court Advocacy Skills and Techniques	3 credits
1-38) Client Counselling and Practice	3 credits
1-39) Research Methodology and Senior Project Writing	3 credits
Elective Courses (earn at least 9 credits)	
1-40) Community Legal Education Program	3 credits
1-41) Environmental Law	3 credits
1-42) Financial Law	3 credits
1-43) Criminology	3 credits
1-44) Legislative Drafting and Practice (Clinic Course)	3 credits
1-45) Contract Writing and Practice (Clinic Course)	3 credits
1-46) Negotiation and Practice (Clinic Course)	3 credits
1-47) Rights of Persons with Disabilities I	3 credits
1-48) Rights of Persons with Disabilities II	3 credits
Graduation Path *(choose one)	
1-50) Senior Project and Defense	3 credits
1-50) Legal Internship/Legal Clinic Programs	3 credits
1-50) Exit Exam	3 credits

Note:

PUC Academic Calendar [Nov-Apr: 12 Credits], [Apr-Aug: 12 Credits] and [Aug-Nov: 9 Credits]

* Bachelor of Laws: 130 Credits (43 Courses)

– 215 –

NATIONAL UNIVERSITY OF LAOS
Faculty of Law and Political Science

Master's Programs

I) LL.M. Course (Master of Law): 50 credits

1) Mandatory's Course (26 credits)		
1-1) Civil Law	3 credits	1st Semester
1-2) Criminal Law	3 credits	1st Semester
1-3) Civil Procedural Law	3 credits	2nd Semester
1-4) Criminal Procedural Law	3 credits	2nd Semester
1-5) Law in Majoring of Business and Trade	3 credits	2nd Semester
1-6) Politic	3 credits	3rd Semester
1-7) Constitution Comparatives Study	3 credits	1st Semester
1-8) Comparative Judicial System	3 credits	3rd Semester
1-9) Philosophy of Law	3 credits	1st Semester
2) Electives Course (14 credits)		
2-1) Administration Comparative Study	2 credits	2nd Semester
2-2) Laws on Finance field	2 credits	2nd Semester
2-3) Labour Law	2 credits	3rd Semester
2-4) Environments Law	2 credits	3rd Semester
2-5) Laws on Naturals Resources	2 credits	3rd Semester
2-6) Economics Offences	2 credits	3rd Semester
2-7) ASEAN's Policy	2 credits	3rd Semester
2-8) International Arbitration	2 credits	3rd Semester

2-9) International Criminal Court	2 credits	3rd Semester
2-10) International Private Law	2 credits	3rd Semester
2-11) International Public Law	2 credits	3rd Semester
3) Master Thesis (10 credits)		
3-1) Graduate Writing Seminar	2 credits	4th Semester
3-2) Writing and Defense Thesis	8 credits	4th Semester

II) LL.M. (Master of Law Majoring in Business Law): 47 credits

1) Mandatory's Course (29 credits)		
1-1) Politic	3 credits	1st Semester
1-2) Commercial and International Trade Law	3 credits	1st Semester
1-3) International Tax Law	3 credits	1st Semester
1-4) Advanced Enterprise Law and Business	3 credits	1st Semester
1-5) Advanced Intellectual Property	2 credits	1st Semester
1-6) Law on Financial Institutions	3 credits	2nd Semester
1-7) Advanced International Economic Cooperation	2 credits	2nd Semester
1-8) Economic and Trade Disputed Resolution	3 credits	2nd Semester
1-9) Advanced Business Economic	2 credits	2nd Semester
1-10) English for Business Law	2 credits	3rd Semester
1-11) Statistic for Academic Research	2 credits	3rd Semester
1-12) Research Methodology	2 credits	2nd Semester
2) Electives Course (4 credits)		
2-1) Insurance Law	2 credits	3rd Semester
2-2) Business and Personal Administration	2 credits	3rd Semester

2-3) Economic Crimes	2 credits	3rd Semester
2-4) Environments Law	2 credits	3rd Semester
2-5) Business Contract	2 credits	3rd Semester
3) Thesis	14 credits	4th Semester

III) Master of Political Science Majoring in Administrative Law: 48 credits

1) Mandatory's Course (30 credits)		
1-1) Policy of Lao PDR	2 credits	1st Semester
1-2) English Language	2 credits	1st Semester
1-3) Constitution Law	3 credits	1st Semester
1-4) Administrative Law	4 credits	1st Semester
1-5) Comparative Administrative Law	2 credits	2nd Semester
1-6) International Relations	2 credits	2nd Semester
1-7) Public Financial Law	2 credits	2nd Semester
1-8) Research Methodology	3 credits	2nd Semester
1-9) Organization Administration	3 credits	3rd Semester
1-10) Public Administration	3 credits	2nd Semester
1-11) Foreign Policy of Laos	2 credits	1st Semester
1-12) Administrative Procedural Law	3 credits	3rd Semester
2) Electives Course (4 credits)		
2-1) ASEAN Study	2 credits	3rd Semester
2-2) Political Science Theory	2 credits	3rd Semester
2-3) Advanced Civil Procedural Law	2 credits	3rd Semester
2-4) Advanced Criminal Procedural Law	2 credits	3rd Semester

COURSE CATALOGS: NATIONAL UNIVERSITY OF LAOS

2-5) International Law	2 credits	3rd Semester
2-6) Environment Law	2 credits	3rd Semester
2-8) International economic Law	2 credits	3rd Semester
2-9) Administrative Court	2 credits	3rd Semester
3) Master Thesis	14 credits	4th Semester

IV) Master of International Law (study in French): 49 credits

1) Mandatory's Course (30 credits)		
1-1) Politic 2 credits	2 credits	1st Semester
1-2) International Private Law (1)	2 credits	1st Semester
1-3) International private Law (2)	1 credits	1st Semester
1-4) International Public Law (1)	2 credits	1st Semester
1-5) International Public Law (2)	1 credits	1st Semester
1-6) French Terminology (1)	2 credits	2nd Semester
1-7) International Trade Law (1)	2 credits	2nd Semester
1-8) International Trade Law (2)	1 credits	2nd Semester
1-9) Comparative Law	2 credits	2nd Semester
1-10) International Arbitration	2 credits	3rd Semester
1-11) ASEAN laws	2 credits	2nd Semester
1-12) EUROPEAN Laws	2 credits	2nd Semester
1-13) International Economic Law (1)	2 credits	3rd Semester
1-14) International Economic Law (2)	1 credits	3rd Semester
1-15) Academic Research and Writing	2 credits	3rd Semester
1-16) French for Legal Study (1)	2 credits	2nd Semester

1-17) French for Legal Study (2)	2 credits	3rd Semester
2) Electives Course (4 credits)		
2-1) Geopolitics	2 credits	1st Semester
2-2) International Humanitarian Law	2 credits	3rd Semester
3) Master Thesis	15 credits	4th Semester

Note:
The First Semester started from October and end in February.
The Second Semester started from March and end in July.
The Third Semester started from August and end in December.
The Fourth Semester started from January and end in May.

* There are two – year course with two different periods of commencement, either in October or in March.
There are five – month in each semester.

COURSE CATALOGS: THAMMASAT UNIVERSITY

THAMMASAT UNIVERSITY, THAILAND
Faculty of Law

LL.M. Courses
(Master of Laws Program in Business Law (English Program))

1) Compulsory Courses	
1-1) Advanced Contracts and Torts Law	3 credits
1-2) Corporate Law	3 credits
1-3) International Business Transactions	3 credits
1-4) Law on Business Finance	3 credits
1-5) Research Methodology	3 credits
2) Elective Courses	
2-1) Selected Legal Problems on Information Technology and Cyberspace	3 credits
2-2) Intellectual Property Law	3 credits
2-3) Alternative Dispute Resolution	3 credits
2-4) International Transportation Law	3 credits
2-5) Insurance Law and Risk Management	3 credits
2-6) Taxation	3 credits
2-7) Competition Law	3 credits
2-8) International Economic Law	3 credits
2-9) Bankruptcy and Debt Restructuring Law	3 credits
2-10) Labor Law and Social Security	3 credits
2-11) Human Rights Law	3 credits
2-12) Advanced Environmental Law	3 credits

– 221 –

2-13) Consumer Protection Law	3 credits
2-14) Advanced Administrative Law	3 credits
2-15) Advanced Criminal Law	3 credits
2-16) Philosophy of Law	3 credits
2-17) Business Law Seminar	3 credits
2-18) Comparative Law of Civil Procedure and Evidence	3 credits
2-19) Independent Study	6 credits
2-20) Thesis	15 credits
3) Choose one of these two courses (Plan A or Plan B)	
3-1) Plan A: Thesis	15 credits
3-2) Plan B: Independent Study	6 credits

Notes:

The requirements for Plan A and Plan B are as follows.

Plan A: Compulsory Courses   15 credits
          Elective Courses   9 credits
          Thesis   15 credits

Plan B: Compulsory Courses   15 credits
          Elective Courses   18 credits
          Independent Study   6 credits

LL.B. Courses

(Bachelor of Laws Program in Business Law (International Program))

1) Compulsory Courses	
1-1) Introduction to Law and Legal Systems	3 credits
1-2) Juristic Acts and Contracts	3 credits
1-3) Skills in Legal Language: Research Writing and Presentation	3 credits
1-4) Obligations: General Principles	3 credits

1-5) Wrongful Acts, Management of Affairs Without Mandate and Undue Enrichment	3 credits
1-6) Property Law	3 credits
1-7) Principles of Criminal Law	3 credits
1-8) Introduction to Public Law	3 credits
1-9) Constitutional Law	3 credits
1-10) Legal Methodology	3 credits
1-11) General Principles of Procedural Law	3 credits
1-12) Public International Law	4 credits
1-13) Philosophy of Law	2 credits
1-14) Legal Profession	2 credits
2) Elective Courses	
2-1) Drafting Contracts and Legal Documents	3 credits
2-2) Secured Transactions	3 credits
2-3) Specific Contracts	4 credits
2-4) Introduction to Public Economic Law	3 credits
2-5) Law on Business Organizations	3 credits
2-6) Consumer Protection Law	3 credits
2-7) Law on Negotiable Instruments	3 credits
2-8) Insurance Law and Practice	3 credits
2-9) Law on Securities and Exchange	3 credits
2-10) Competition Law	3 credits
2-11) Intellectual Property Law	3 credits
2-12) Income Tax Law	3 credits
2-13) Business Law Seminar	3 credits

2-14) Accounting Principles and Financial Statements for Lawyers	3 credits
2-15) Customs Law and Global Trade	3 credits
2-16) Consumption Tax Law	3 credits
2-17) Property Tax Law	3 credits
2-18) Banking and Finance Law	3 credits
2-19) Labor Law	3 credits
2-20) Natural Resource and Environmental Law for Business	3 credits
2-21) Law on Information Technology	3 credits
2-22) Law on Mass Communication and Telecommunication Business	3 credits
2-23) Insolvency Law	3 credits
2-24) Private International Law	3 credits
2-25) International Environmental Law	3 credits
2-26) European Union Law	3 credits
2-27) Law on Real Estate Development	3 credits
2-28) Law on International Business Transactions	3 credits
2-29) Alternative Dispute Resolutions for Business	3 credits
2-30) Copyright Law	3 credits
2-31) Patent Law	3 credits
2-32) Trademark Law	3 credits
2-33) International and Comparative Intellectual Property Law	3 credits
2-34) Maritime Law	3 credits

COURSE CATALOGS: THAMMASAT UNIVERSITY

2-35) Comparative Business Law	3 credits
2-36) Introduction to International Tax Law	3 credits
2-37) Taxation Theories and Tax Policies	3 credits
2-38) Principles of Tax Accounting	3 credits
2-39) Tax Disputes Settlement	3 credits
2-40) Administration of Taxation and Tax Planning	3 credits
2-41) Legal Internship	3 credits
2-42) International Trade Law	3 credits
2-43) International Investment Law	3 credits
2-44) International Monetary and Financial Law	3 credits
2-45) ASEAN Law	3 credits
2-46) Comparative Economic Community Law	3 credits
2-47) Basic Legal Writing Skills	3 credits
2-48) Private Law Seminar	3 credits
2-49) Introduction to the American Legal System	3 credits
2-50) Introduction to the Chinese Legal law	3 credits
2-51) Introduction to the English Legal System	3 credits
2-52) Introduction to the French Legal System	3 credits
2-53) Introduction to the German legal System	3 credits
2-54) Introduction to the Japanese Legal System	3 credits
2-55) Judicial Systems and Procedure	3 credits
2-56) Family Law	3 credits

2-57) Law of Succession	3 credits
2-58) Economic Analysis of Law	3 credits
2-59) Evolution of the Legal Systems	3 credits
2-60) Medical Law	3 credits
2-61) Law of Evidence	3 credits
2-62) Human Rights and Citizen Rights	3 credits
2-63) Law of the Sea	3 credits
2-64) Comparative Private Law	3 credits
2-65) Current Legal Issues	3 credits
2-66) International Law for Development	3 credits
2-67) Moot Court	3 credits

COURSE CATALOGS: UNIVERSITY OF YANGON

UNIVERSITY OF YANGON, MYANMAR
Department of Law

LL.M. Course
(Master of Laws): 64 credits

1) Civil Law		
1-1) Criminal Law	4 credits	1st Semester
1-2) Law of Business Organizations	4 credits	1st Semester
1-3) Myanmar Customary Law I	4 credits	1st Semester
1-4) Constitutional Law I	4 credits	1st Semester
1-5) Criminal Procedure	4 credits	2nd Semester
1-6) Civil Litigation	4 credits	2nd Semester
1-7) Family Laws	4 credits	2nd Semester
1-8) Constitutional Law II	4 credits	2nd Semester
1-9) Special Criminal Laws	4 credits	3rd Semester
1-10) Law of Evidence	4 credits	3rd Semester
1-11) Labour Law	4 credits	3rd Semester
1-12) Land Law	4 credits	3rd Semester
1-13) Master Thesis (16 credits)		
(a) Research and Seminar	8 credits	4th Semester
(b) Thesis and Viva Voice	8 credits	4th Semester
2) International Law		
2-1) Public International Law I	4 credits	1st Semester
2-2) International Economic Law	4 credits	1st Semester
2-3) International Law of Armed Conflict	4 credits	1st Semester

– 227 –

2-4) Law of Treaties	4 credits	1st Semester
2-5) Public International Law II	4 credits	2nd Semester
2-6) Law of International Trade	4 credits	2nd Semester
2-7) International Humanitarian Law	4 credits	2nd Semester
2-8) International Environmental Law	4 credits	2nd Semester
2-9) Law of International Institutions	4 credits	3rd Semester
2-10) International Air and Space Law	4 credits	3rd Semester
2-11) Law of the Sea	4 credits	3rd Semester
2-12) Intellectual Property Law	4 credits	3rd Semester
2-13) Master Thesis (16 credits)		
(a) Research and Seminar	8 credits	4th Semester
(b) Thesis and Viva Voice	8 credits	4th Semester

3) Maritime Law

3-1) Marine Insurance I	4 credits	1st Semester
3-2) Carriage of Goods by Sea I	4 credits	1st Semester
3-3) Maritime Law I	4 credits	1st Semester
3-4) Law of the Sea I	4 credits	1st Semester
3-5) Marine Insurance II	4 credits	2nd Semester
3-6) Carriage of Goods by Sea II	4 credits	2nd Semester
3-7) Maritime Law II	4 credits	2nd Semester
3-8) Law of the Sea II	4 credits	2nd Semester
3-9) Marine Insurance III	4 credits	3rd Semester
3-10) Carriage of Goods by Sea III	4 credits	3rd Semester
3-11) Maritime Law III	4 credits	3rd Semester
3-12) Law of the Sea III	4 credits	3rd Semester

COURSE CATALOGS: UNIVERSITY OF YANGON

3-13) Master Thesis (16 credits)		
(a) Research and Seminar	8 credits	4th Semester
(b) Thesis and Viva Voice	8 credits	4th Semester
4) Commercial Law		
4-1) Law of Business Organizations	4 credits	1st Semester
4-2) International Economic Law	4 credits	1st Semester
4-3) Investment Laws and Law of Arbitration	4 credits	1st Semester
4-4) Law of Taxation	4 credits	1st Semester
4-5) Transport Laws	4 credits	2nd Semester
4-6) Private International Law	4 credits	2nd Semester
4-7) Law of Employment	4 credits	2nd Semester
4-8) Banking and Finance Law	4 credits	2nd Semester
4-9) General Insurance	4 credits	3rd Semester
4-10) Law of International Trade	4 credits	3rd Semester
4-11) Environmental Law	4 credits	3rd Semester
4-12) Intellectual Property Law	4 credits	3rd Semester
4-13) Master Thesis (16 credits)		
(a) Research and Seminar	8 credits	4th Semester
(b) Thesis and Viva Voice	8 credits	4th Semester

LL.B. Course

(Bachelor of Laws): 204 credits

1) First Year (40 credits)

(a) Foundation Courses (12 credits)		
1-1) Myanmar	3 credits	1st Semester
1-2) Myanmar	3 credits	2nd Semester
1-3) English	3 credits	1st Semester
1-4) English	3 credits	2nd Semester
(b) Core Courses (22 credits)		
1-5) Introduction to The Study of Law I	4 credits	1st Semester
1-6) History of State and Law	4 credits	1st Semester
1-7) Aspects of Myanmar	3 credits	1st Semester
1-8) Introduction to The Study of Law II	4 credits	2nd Semester
1-9) Jurisprudence	4 credits	2nd Semester
1-10) Aspects of Myanmar	3 credits	2nd Semester
(c) Elective Courses (6 credits) (Other Specializations) (one subject to be taken for one semester)		
1-11) Logic in Practice I	3 credits	1st Semester
1-12) Introduction to Myanmar Civilizations I	3 credits	1st Semester
1-13) Introduction to International Relations I	3 credits	1st Semester
1-14) Public Relations	3 credits	1st Semester
1-15) Principles of Microeconomics	3 credits	1st Semester
1-16) Geography of Southeast Asian Countries	3 credits	1st Semester
1-17) Buddhist Culture	3 credits	1st Semester
1-18) Logic in Practice II	3 credits	2nd Semester

COURSE CATALOGS: UNIVERSITY OF YANGON

1-19) Introduction to Myanmar Civilizations II	3 credits	2nd Semester
1-20) Introduction to International Relations II	3 credits	2nd Semester
1-21) Understanding Human Interaction	3 credits	2nd Semester
1-22) Principles of Macroeconomics	3 credits	2nd Semester
1-23) Geography of Myanmar	3 credits	2nd Semester
1-24) Pali Literature	3 credits	2nd Semester

2) Second Year (42 credits)

(a) Foundation Course (6 credits)		
2-1) English	3 credits	1st Semester
2-2) English	3 credits	2nd Semester
(b) Core Courses (24 credits)		
2-3) Myanmar Customary Law I	4 credits	1st Semester
2-4) Law of Contract	4 credits	1st Semester
2-5) Labour Law	4 credits	1st Semester
2-6) Myanmar Customary Law II	4 credits	2nd Semester
2-7) Law of Tort	4 credits	2nd Semester
2-8) Land Law	4 credits	2nd Semester
(c) Elective Courses (12 credits) Law Specialization (one law subject to be taken for one semester)		
2-9) Law Relating to Sale of Goods	3 credits	1st Semester
2-10) Principles of Legal Profession	3 credits	1st Semester
2-11) Negotiable Instruments Act	3 credits	2nd Semester
2-12) Law of Banking	3 credits	2nd Semester
Other Specializations (one subject to be taken for one semester)		

2-13) Developing Communicative Skills I	3 credits	1st Semester
2-14) Philosophy of Law I	3 credits	1st Semester
2-15) Elements of Political Institutions I	3 credits	1st Semester
2-16) Macroeconomics	3 credits	1st Semester
2-17) Developing Communicative Skills II	3 credits	2nd Semester
2-18) Philosophy of Law II	3 credits	2nd Semester
2-19) Elements of Political Institutions II	3 credits	2nd Semester
2-20) International Trade	3 credits	2nd Semester

3) Third Year (42 credits)

(a) Foundation Course: 6 credits		
3-1) English	3 credits	1st Semester
3-2) English	3 credits	2nd Semester
(b) Core Courses: 24 credits		
3-3) Criminal Law	4 credits	1st Semester
3-4) Public International Law	4 credits	1st Semester
3-5) Business Law I	4 credits	1st Semester
3-6) Criminal Procedure Code	4 credits	2nd Semester
3-7) Human Rights Law	4 credits	2nd Semester
3-8) Business Law II	4 credits	2nd Semester
(c) Elective Courses (12 credits) Law Specialization (one subject to be taken)		
3-9) Conflict of Laws	3 credits	1st Semester
3-10) Special Criminal Laws	3 credits	1st Semester
3-11) Law of Insurance	3 credits	2nd Semester

COURSE CATALOGS: UNIVERSITY OF YANGON

3-12) Law of Treaties	3 credits	2nd Semester
Other Specialization (one subject to be taken)		
3-13) Crime and Psychology I (Psychology Specialization)	3 credits	1st Semester
3-14) Developing Communicative Skills I (English Specialization)	3 credits	1st Semester
3-15) Introduction to Economics of Development (Eco Specialization)	3 credits	1st Semester
3-16) Current Issues in International Relations I (International Relations Specialization)	3 credits	1st Semester
3-17) Crime and Psychology II (Psychology Specialization)	3 credits	2nd Semester
3-18) International Finance (Eco Specialization)	3 credits	2nd Semester
3-19) Developing Communicative Skills II (English Specialization)	3 credits	2nd Semester
3-20) Current Issues in International Relations II (International Relations Specialization)	3 credits	2nd Semester

4) Fourth Year (44 credits)

(a) Core Courses (32 credits)		
4-1) Constitutional Law	4 credits	1st Semester
4-2) Civil Procedure Code I	4 credits	1st Semester
4-3) Revenue Law I	4 credits	1st Semester
4-4) Law of International Institutions I	4 credits	1st Semester
4-5) Administrative Law	4 credits	2nd Semester
4-6) Civil Procedure Code II	4 credits	2nd Semester
4-7) Revenue Law II	4 credits	2nd Semester

4-8) Law of International Institutions II	4 credits	2nd Semester

(b) Elective Course (12 credits)

4-9) Environmental Law	3 credits	1st Semester
4-10) International Economic Law	3 credits	1st Semester
4-11) Child Law of Myanmar	3 credits	1st Semester
4-12) Law of the Sea	3 credits	2nd Semester
4-13) Transport Laws	3 credits	2nd Semester
4-14) Intellectual Property Law	3 credits	2nd Semester

5) Fifth Year (36 credits)

(a) Core Courses (24 credits)

5-1) Law of Evidence I	4 credits	1st Semester
5-2) Shipping Law I	4 credits	1st Semester
5-3) Military Law	4 credits	1st Semester
5-4) Law of Evidence II	4 credits	2nd Semester
5-5) Shipping Law II	4 credits	2nd Semester
5-6) Civil Litigation	4 credits	2nd Semester

(b) Elective Courses (12 credits)

5-7) Comparative Law	3 credits	1st Semester
5-8) Criminology	3 credits	1st Semester
5-9) International Humanitarian Law	3 credits	1st Semester
5-10) Constitutions of ASEAN Countries	3 credits	2nd Semester
5-11) Law of Commercial Arbitration	3 credits	2nd Semester
5-12) International Air and Space Law	3 credits	2nd Semester

COURSE CATALOGS: KEIO UNIVERSITY LAW SCHOOL

KEIO UNIVERSITY LAW SCHOOL, JAPAN

LL.M. Course

1) Japanese Law and Asian Law in Global Practical Perspective		
1-1) Law, Culture and Development in Asia	2 credits	Spring
1-2) Introduction to Asian Law	2 credits	Fall
1-3) Japanese Law State and Citizen	2 credits	Spring
1-4) Japanese Law (Administrative Law and Regulatory Policy)	2 credits	Spring
1-5) Japanese Law (Trade Law and Policy)	1 credit	Fall
1-6) Japanese Law (Economy and Social Structure)	2 credits	Fall
1-7) Japanese Law (Legal History and Transformation)	1 credit	Fall
1-8) Japanese Law (Labor and Employment)	1 credit	Fall
1-9) Japanese Law (Contemporary Issues)	2 credits	Fall
1-10) Japanese Law in Cross-border Matters	1 credit	Spring
2) Global Business and Law		
2-1) International Commercial Transactions	2 credits	Fall
2-2) Government Relations and Law	2 credits	Spring
2-3) Cross-border Litigation	2 credits	Spring
2-4) Finance Transactions and Securities Regulations in Japan	2 credits	Fall
2-5) Bankruptcy Laws	2 credits	Fall

2-6) Law, Finance and Taxation of Corporate Acquisitions	2 credits	Spring
2-7) European Integration and Global Business Law	2 credits	Fall
2-8) Corporate Governance and Risk Management	2 credits	Spring
2-9) International Commercial Arbitration I	2 credits	Spring
2-10) International Commercial Arbitration II	2 credits	Fall
2-11) International Investment Arbitration	2 credits	Spring
2-12) Japanese Competition Law	2 credits	Fall
2-13) Business Strategy and Contract	1 credit	Spring
2-14) Law of the Internet	2 credits	Spring
2-15) Start-up Company and Venture Capital Law	2 credits	Fall
2-16) Case Study in International Dispute Resolution	1 credit	Spring

3) Global Security and Law

3-1) International Law	2 credits	Fall
3-2) Law of International Organizations	1 credit	Fall
3-3) Introduction to Global Law	1 credit	Spring
3-4) Globalization and International Human Rights in Asia	1 credit	Fall
3-5) Globalization and International Criminal Law	1 credit	Fall
3-6) International Security Law	1 credit	Fall
3-7) Environmental Law and Disaster	2 credits	Spring
3-8) Introduction to Space Law	2 credits	Spring
3-9) Multinational Corporations and Law	2 credits	Fall

COURSE CATALOGS: KEIO UNIVERSITY LAW SCHOOL

4) Innovations and Intellectual Property Law

4-1) Intellectual Property from a Global Perspective	2 credits	Spring
4-2) Global Intellectual Property Management	2 credits	Spring
4-3) Transnational Intellectual Property Enforcement	2 credits	Spring
4-4) International IP Licensing Agreements	2 credits	Fall

5) Area Studies

5-1) Area Studies of Law (South East Asia)	1 credit	Fall
5-2) Area Studies of Law (EU)	1 credit	Spring

6) Comparative Law

6-1) Introduction to American Law	2 credits	Fall
6-2) Comparative Constitutional Law	2 credits	Spring
6-3) Comparative Contract Law	2 credits	Fall
6-4) Comparative Corporate Law	2 credits	Fall
6-5) Comparative Corporate Finance and Law	2 credits	Fall
6-6) English Contract Law	2 credits	Fall

7) Current Legal Issues

7-1) Art Business and Law	1 credit	Spring
7-2) Sports Law and Dispute Resolution	1 credit	Fall
7-3) Gaming Law	1 credit	Spring
7-4) Seminar (Legal Issues in China, India and ASEAN)	1 credit	Spring
7-5) Seminar (Comparative Patent Case Law and Litigation)	1 credit	Spring
7-6) Seminar (Case Study in International Competition Law)	1 credit	Spring

7-7) Seminar (International Dispute Resolution in Asia)	1 credit	Spring
7-8) Seminar (Global Tax Perspectives)	1 credit	Spring
8) Legal Research and Writing		
8-1) Graduate Writing Seminar	2 credits	Spring
8-2) 8-3) Research Paper I, Research Paper II	2 credits	Spring / Fall
9) Practical Training		
9-1) Negotiation	2 credits	Spring
9-2) Arbitration	2 credits	Fall
9-3) Drafting International Agreements	2 credits	Fall
9-4) Drafting and Negotiation of M&A and JV Transactions	2 credits	Fall
9-5) Moot Court I	2 credits	Spring / Fall
9-7) Moot Court II	2 credits	Spring / Fall
9-8) Internship	2 credits	Spring / Fall

INDEX

A

absolute right   177
academic calendar   91, 114, 137
accommodations   17, 20, 128
admission   54
ASEAN   34, 161
ASEAN Credit Transfer System (ACTS)
    138, 142
ASEAN Economic Community (AEC)   8,
    35
ASEAN Law Association   37
ASEAN University Network (AUN)   19,
    62, 65, 96, 138
ASEAN University Network-Southeast Asia
    Engineering Education Development
    Network (AUN-SEED/Net)   96
Asian Law Institute (ASLI)   35
Asian laws   6
assessment   73

B

bar examination   73, 105

C

case law   163, 168
civil law system   123
clinical legal education   98
collaboration   50, 69
common law system   123
comparative law   4, 7, 41, 156
comparative legal analysis   124
comparative legal education   185
credit points   15, 18, 140
credit transfer   15, 72, 77, 91, 141, 152

culture   89
curriculum   74

D

degree programs   9
distance learning   117
double degree program   10, 115

E

EU - SHARE   63
exchange of students   44
exchange of teachers   43
externship   57

F

faculty exchange programs   32
financial expenses   127
French legal concepts   45

G

global governance   9
globalization of legal education   21
good governance   9
good practice   53
grade point   15, 18
grading system   75

H

higher education institutions (HEIs)   83
human legal resources   185
Human Resource Development Program
    (HRD)   95

I

inbound exchange   108
in-depth knowledge of foreign law   4
intensive teaching   150
international collaboration   27, 86
international exchange program   49, 72, 87, 97, 137
international trade law   161
internationalisation   25
internationalism   48
internship   57
inter-university courses   147

J

JASSO   132
joint program   140
Juris Doctor   104

L

language barrier   16, 19, 124
law and development   5
lecture   122
legal clinic   49
legal culture   36
legal education   3, 18, 93, 110
legal practice   5
legal syllogism   172
legal theory   4

M

Massive Open Online Courses (MOOCs)   37
MOA   51, 62, 93
MOU   49, 62, 93
multidisciplinarism   48
non-degree programs   11

O

obstacles   71, 72, 137
outbound exchange   111

P

pedagogical methods   170
pioneerism   48
practical training   117
precedent   174
pro bono   99

R

recurrent education   110
research paper   45

S

scholarship   99
semester system   70
seminar style   122
short-term program   139
Socratic method   122
spirit of law   5
student exchange programs   30, 88
study law abroad   3
Summer Seminar   13, 161
sustainable development   22

T

teaching methodology   121
teaching methods   122
tuition fees   17, 131

U

United Nations Development Programme (UNDP)   98

V

Vietnamese legal concepts   45
visa   54

W

WTO   162

ABOUT KEIGLAD

KEIGLAD - Keio Institute for Global Law and Development

Keio Institute for Global Law and Development (KEIGLAD) was established for the purpose of assisting the promotion of international exchange and international cooperation among researchers, students, and staffs for legal study and legal education. KEIGLAD will promote the concerned projects as follow:

- Promotion of the Program for Asian Global Legal Professions (PAGLEP)
- Collection of information on the concerned comparative law
- Collection of information on the method of legal education
- Provision of materials for legal education
- Provision of information and support for foreign students who will study at Keio Law School and Keio Law School students who will study abroad
- Promotion of the concerned symposiums and research meetings
- Publication of working papers
- Other matters concerned with objectives of KEIGLAD

Through these activities, KEIGLAD aims to contribute to the promotion of "Law-Ubiquitous Society", in which Anyone can access to justice Anywhere and Anytime.

ABOUT THE AUTHORS

Naoya Katayama
Former Dean, Professor, Keio University Law School, Japan

Isao Kitai
Dean, Professor, Keio University Law School, Japan

Hiroshi Matsuo
Director, KEIGLAD; Professor, Keio University Law School, Japan

Vu Thi Lan Anh
Vice Rector, Associate Professor, Hanoi Law University, Vietnam

Nguyen Van Quang
Associate Professor, Hanoi Law University, Vietnam

Nguyen Ngoc Dien
Vice-Rector, Professor, the Vietnam National University of Economics and Law in Ho Chi Minh City, Vietnam

Le Van Hinh
Deputy Head of UEL's International Relations Office, the Vietnam National University of Economics and Law in Ho Chi Minh City, Vietnam

Kong Phallack
Dean, Professor, Faculty of Law and Public Affairs, Paññāsāstra University of Cambodia

Phin Sovath
Assistant Dean, Professor, Faculty of Law and Public Affairs, Paññāsāstra University of Cambodia

Viengvilay Thiengchanhxay
Dean, Associate Professor, Faculty of Law and Political Science, National University of Laos

Sonenaly Nanthavong
Head of International Cooperation Unit, Faculty of Law and Political Science, National University of Laos

Junavit Chalidabhongse
Assistant Dean, Deputy Director of International Programs, Faculty of Law, Thammasat University, Thailand

Viravat Chantachote
Assistant Professor, Chairman of the Curriculum Development and Quality Assurance in Education, Faculty of Law, Thammasat University, Thailand

Khin Chit Chit
Professor, Department of Law, University of Yangon, Myanmar

Khin Phone Myint Kyu
Professor, Department of Law, University of Yangon, Myanmar

David G. Litt
Professor, Keio University Law School, Japan

Susumu Masuda
Professor, Keio University Law School, Japan

Hitomi Fukasawa
Researcher, KEIGLAD, Japan

Mao Kimpav
Manager of Administration and Law Programs, Faculty of Law and Public Affairs, Paññāsāstra University of Cambodia

MEXT/JSPS Re-Inventing Japan Project (Type B: ASEAN) FY 2016
文部科学省　平成 28 年度大学の世界展開力事業（ASEAN 地域における大学間交流の推進）
タイプ B 採択プログラム

Challenges for Studying Law Abroad in the Asian Region
Programs for Asian Global Legal Professions Series II

2018 年 2 月 23 日　初版第 1 刷発行

編　者―――――KEIGLAD
発行者―――――KEIGLAD
　　　　　　　（慶應義塾大学大学院法務研究科グローバル法研究所）
　　　　　　　代表者　松尾　弘
　　　　　　　〒 108-8345　東京都港区三田 2-15-45
　　　　　　　TEL 03-5427-1574
発売所―――――慶應義塾大学出版会株式会社
　　　　　　　〒 108-8346　東京都港区三田 2-19-30
　　　　　　　TEL 03-3451-3584　FAX 03-3451-3122
装　丁―――――鈴木　衛
組　版―――――株式会社 STELLA
印刷・製本――株式会社丸井工文社
カバー印刷――株式会社太平印刷社

©2018　KEIGLAD
Printed in Japan ISBN978-4-7664-2504-8
落丁・乱丁本はお取替致します。